"Practical and incredibly insightful...a go-to book for dads of daughters. This is stuff I can immediately incorporate in relating to my three daughters... Hint: Moms, buy this book for your husband!"

—**Jim Burns,** president of HomeWord
and author of *Teenology* and *Confident Parenting*

"In easy-to-swallow and to-the-point snippets, Jay gives dads fantastic advice. This is a great tool for any father who wants to be intentional about raising whole and healthy children in a culture that makes that task difficult."

—**Dannah Gresh,** author of *Six Ways to Keep the "Little" in Your Girl*
and *Six Ways to Keep the "Good" in Your Boy*

"Every dad wants his daughter to grow up with dignity, self-respect, grace, humility, virtue, and significance...Jay's approach helps dads with the development of these desirable character traits from early childhood through walking them down the aisle."

—**Darrel Billups,** executive director of
the National Coalition of Ministries to Men

"Jay provides dads with a wealth of insights and practical ideas that will help them invest wisely in their daughters' lives...in a way that allows dads to smile and get rid of the fright. He instills confidence that you can have a close and difference-making relationship with your daughter."

—**Carey Casey,** CEO of the National Center for Fathering,
radio host of *Today's Father*, and author of *Championship Fathering*

"What a wise and wonderful book!...Be sure you give copies to every father of a daughter. He will rise up and call you blessed. His daughters will too!"

—**Steve Brown,** popular author,
seminary professor, and radio teacher on *Key Life*

"Dads have the unique opportunity to influence, guide, and encourage their daughters to grow into godly and gracious young ladies...*52 Things Daughters Need from Their Dads* is a playbook that gives a father the tools he can use for building a lasting and loving relationship."

—**Karol Ladd,** bestselling author of *The Power of a Positive Mom*

"Payleitner has done it again! Each section of this treasure chest of wisdom contains insights on what every daughter needs from her daddy, and tips every man needs to think about—all in an easy-to-read format. Well done, my friend!"

—**Rick Johnson,** bestselling author of
Better Dads, Stronger Sons and *That's My Girl*

"Helpful not only because it reminds us of the priority our daughters should have in our lives—it also gives us creative, useful ideas for how to create an unbreakable bond with them. Thanks, Jay, for your heart to help all of us dads!"

—**Wayne Shepherd,** national Christian radio host of
First Person with Wayne Shepherd

52 THINGS DAUGHTERS NEED FROM THEIR DADS

JAY PAYLEITNER

HARVEST HOUSE PUBLISHERS
EUGENE, OREGON

Cover by Left Coast Design, Portland, Oregon

Cover photo © Oskin Pavel / Shutterstock

Jay Payleitner is represented by MacGregor Literary Inc. of Hillsboro, Oregon.

52 THINGS DAUGHTERS NEED FROM THEIR DADS
Copyright © 2013 by Jay Payleitner
Published by Harvest House Publishers
Eugene, Oregon 97402
www.harvesthousepublishers.com

Library of Congress Cataloging-in-Publication Data
    Payleitner, Jay K.
    52 things daughters need from their dads / Jay Payleitner.
       p. cm.
    ISBN 978-0-7369-4810-4 (pbk.)
    ISBN 978-0-7369-4811-1 (eBook)
    1. Fathers and daughters—Religious aspects—Christianity. I. Title. II. Title: Fifty-two things daughters need from their dads.
    BV4529.17.P385 2013
    248.8'421—dc23

                                          2012033730

Printed in the United States of America

13 14 15 16 17 18 19 20 21 / BP-CD / 10 9 8 7 6 5 4

To my Rae Anne.
You brighten each day.

Acknowledgments

First, of course, to our heavenly Father. Above all.

Then, I must credit most of the dads I know for doing a spectacular job. Your daughters are growing into wonderful young women exhibiting grace, wisdom, and integrity. Some of these men even helped shape the content of this book. That includes Chuck Thomas, Scott Kirk, Paul Gossard, Dave George, Ray Ochromowicz, Jon Gauger, Bob Miller, Terry Schweizer, and Mark Payleitner.

Other dads of daughters who contributed more indirectly are Len Asquini, Tim Coleman, Dwight Curran, Dave Buckman, Rudy DePolo, Brad Dennison, Todd Winkler, Josh McDowell, Dennis O'Malley, and Tim Hollinger. Watching these men interact with their daughters has been a tremendously valuable learning experience. I recommend you also spend intentional time with other dads who are putting in the extra effort to get it right.

Thanks to all those rooting specifically for this project. That includes Sandra Bishop, my visionary agent at MacGregor Literary; Carey Casey and Brock Griffin at the National Center for Fathering; and Terry Glaspey, Bob Hawkins Jr., and the entire talented team at Harvest House Publishers.

I'm assuredly grateful to the pastors and event planners who have invited me to encourage, laugh with, and challenge diverse throngs of dads and husbands. It's always fun and always humbling.

Love and thanks to my bride, Rita, and my three lovely daughters-in-law, Rachel, Lindsay, and Megan. I'm still learning how to be the husband and father-in-law you deserve.

And finally, to my remarkable, unforgettable, tenacious, and sweet Rae Anne...xxxo.

Contents

FOREWORD

by Robin Brown DeMurga,
daughter of Steve Brown
(author and founder of Key Life Network)

Although there is no such thing as a perfect father and only God can fill that role, daughters need their earthly fathers…desperately. You may not think of yourself this way, but you are God's gift to your daughter. And it's clear you want to be the best father you can be. You want to love your daughter well. (After all, you picked up this book, right?)

My own father did the best he could. That's all any of us can do as we maneuver through life. Sure, you *want* to be a better dad, but you are always going to fall short and feel a little guilty when your perfect kids don't turn out so perfect. Thankfully, God's grace always makes up for our lack.

For me, life as a PK ("Preacher's Kid") was hard. What kid stands a chance competing with God and God's work? Dad was, for the most part, an absentee father…and he would be the first to admit it. In recent years, we've come to terms with our daddy–daughter relationship and have had great conversations filled not so much with regrets, but a new appreciation for God's faithfulness, forgiveness, and our own human limitations.

There is nothing like time and maturity—all by God's grace—to enable us to finally see our parents as the struggling human beings they were and are. And in the case of my dad and me, working side by side at Key Life Network has literally forced healing, reconciliation, and growth.

The memories I do have of Dad from my growing-up years are

strong ones that I cherish. A father–daughter lunch date at IHOP with chocolate-chip pancakes and a chocolate milkshake (that still sounds like a great meal to me!). As a teenager, lots of bedroom-door-slamming on my part with Dad frantic and frustrated, but caring immeasurably, on the other side. When we first moved to Miami from Boston, Dad's first attempt at breaking open a coconut using just about every tool imaginable—with all of us laughing and keeping our distance (for the record, a hammer and nail did the trick). Dad fiercely going to bat for me with a high-school English teacher (I was so embarrassed!). And at age five— with Mom's urging and only after my passing what seemed like a theological pop quiz (he didn't think a child that young could understand salvation)—Dad gently guiding me into a relationship with Jesus…as I sat on my bed, folded my hands, and prayed alongside him.

In spite of my dad's lacks, my sister and I never doubted his unconditional love for us. He told us often and repeatedly how much he loved us and how proud he was of us. He also humbly apologized whenever he was wrong or neglectful (he still does to this day).

And now Dad and I are both a lot older, my growing-up years are long over, and God has given me a new perspective on just how much my father was able to build into my life.

As I read the book you hold, Jay Payleitner's *52 Things Daughters Need from Their Dads*, I nodded my head over and over as I laughed and cried. You'll find here solid suggestions—all practical, all doable, many crazy fun, and many surprising and brand-new—for being the best father you can be.

And even when you fail or fall short, God's grace will make up for your lack. Isn't that a relief?

Always Daddy's Little Girl

Look back at the photo on the front cover of this book. What do you think?

(For the record, it's not me and it's not my daughter, Rae Anne. I don't have that much hair. And Rae is 20.)

I lobbied my publisher hard for a cover photo featuring a father and his daughter right around 12 years old. Because dads fear that age. Don't we?

For her entire life, our sweet little girl has been worshiping her daddy. Anything we say, she believes. Anyplace we go, she wants to tag along. Anytime she's scared or hurting, all we have to do is show up and all the bad stuff melts away.

We like being the daddy of a little girl. It's really pretty easy. And great fun. But we also know that magic won't last.

Change is coming. And we don't know what our relationship is going to look like on the other side. We've heard ominous stories of teenage girls raging against their fathers. We feel helpless when we consider the world she's about to enter. We imagine the worst: sexual promiscuity, eating disorders, alcohol, drugs, depression, obsessing over looks, sleepless nights, parties she isn't invited to, parties she is invited to, homework assignments we can't begin to help with, and whether or not we matter anymore.

In the debate about what photo best paints the father–daughter picture, the editorial and design team at Harvest House Publishers made an excellent point. *No matter what age she really is, we always see our daughter as our little girl.*

I must say, I had to agree.

Rae Anne has four older brothers. All out of college. Three of them even married. But the dominant mental images I carry in my head of Alec, Randall, Max, and Isaac are of their coming-of-age season in middle school or high school.

Rae Anne is a beautiful, strong, dedicated, fierce, and fabulous young woman. But...sorry, Rae. You will always be my little girl.

Dad, fear not. Stop imagining the worst. You and your daughter will be fine. Better than fine. With a little prayer and preparation, your future will be filled with good conversation, lively debates, some tears, much laughter, quick hugs, longer hugs, a few sleepless nights, some grand celebrations, and memories that sweep you into the next stage of life for you and your family.

I must warn you that some of the chapters in this book do contain cautionary tales and warning signs to watch for. But anticipating what might be lurking around the next corner is part of what you signed up for as a dad.

Most important, I hope this book will help you realize you're not alone in this adventure called "raising a daughter." Every situation is different, but there are certainly quite a few friends and family members cheering you on. And, God himself gave you that little girl to love, protect, and provide for. His plan for you and your family is rock solid. Count on it.

> *"Certain is it that there is no kind of affection so purely*
> *angelic as of a father to a daughter. In love to our wives*
> *there is desire; to our sons, ambition; but to our daughters*
> *there is something which there are no words to express."*
>
> —Joseph Addison

A Daughter Needs Her Dad...

To Be the Perfect Father

Your daughter needs a father she can count on 100 percent of the time. With 100 percent perfect advice. Infinite vision into the future. Providing for her every need. Available 24/7/365. This is what you might call an imperative. A must-have. An absolute life requirement.

To relieve any pressure you might now be feeling, let me say this: "Dad, that ain't you. No one expects you to be a perfect father."

For sure, you love your little girl 100 percent of the time. But that's not enough. You are going to make mistakes. You are going to set expectations that are impossible to meet. You are going to get angry at things that are really not a big deal. You are going to give her things she does not need and cause her to miss opportunities she should have. You are going to open the wrong doors and close the wrong windows. You are going to be silent when she needs to hear you say, "I love you" or "I'm sorry." You are not and cannot be the perfect father.

You probably already know where this is going.

Since you can't be the perfect father, you'll be glad to know that your daughter has a Father in heaven who is exactly that.

He does have a perfect plan for your daughter. "'I know the plans I have for you,' declares the LORD, 'plans to prosper you and not to harm you, plans to give you hope and a future'" (Jeremiah 29:11).

He will never leave her stranded. "Surely I am with you always, to the very end of the age" (Matthew 28:20).

But wait. If God is all the father your daughter really needs, then what in blue blazes is your job? Are you an afterthought? Are you a fraud, an imitation? Are you superfluous? Redundant? Nonessential?

Of course not. You're not God. But you are a dad. Just like Joseph filled the role of husband to Mary and father to Jesus, you've got a job to do. Like Abraham trusted God's plan for Isaac (Genesis 22). Like Jairus wept for his dying daughter and sought out Jesus' help (Mark 5). The Bible acknowledges and has all kinds of clear instructions for earthly fathers. Don't exasperate your kids (Ephesians 6:4). Manage your household (1 Timothy 3:4). Discipline your children (Proverbs 19:18). Look for teachable moments with your kids (Deuteronomy 6:7). Love your wife (Ephesians 5:25).

So yes, Dad. You have a job to do. Even though you can't be the perfect father she needs, you are the best she has right now. And can I say, Dad, you're doing a pretty good job? The fact that you're still plowing through this first chapter of a book with a title like this is a good indication of what's in your heart and your deep desire to be the father your daughter needs.

There's an oft-told story that might help you embrace your role.

> A sweet little girl who looks a lot like your daughter is frightened by the crashes and flashes of a thunderstorm. From her bed she calls out to her daddy. He comes in with a gentle smile and sits down on the edge of her bed, assuring his daughter that she need not be afraid—she is safe and Jesus is always with her. The little girl thinks about that idea for a moment and then says, "I know that, Daddy. But right now, I need someone with skin on."

You're not God. But to your daughter, your physical presence—your words, actions, hugs, provision, and example—is part of God's big design for raising a woman of virtue and achievement.

Years from now, you'll look back and see that even during times when you didn't know what to do or how to respond in a crisis, your presence was all that was really needed. You may have felt like you didn't do enough. But to your daughter, you represented "God with skin on."

Takeaway

Too many fathers beat themselves up or neglect their fathering duties because they don't always know the right thing to do or the right words to say. It's really okay. Join the club. Making mistakes is part of being a dad. In the meantime, make sure your little girl is growing in relationship with her perfect heavenly Father.

> *"If you…though you are evil, know how to give good gifts to your children, how much more will your Father in heaven give good gifts to those who ask him!"*
>
> —Jesus, in Matthew 7:11

A Daughter Needs Her Dad...

To Do Stuff with Her Only

I don't know how many kids you have. But you should make it a point to do something at least once a month with each one of your kids by themselves. Just you and them. With a son, you can call it whatever you want. "Man time." "Palling around." "Dadapalooza." But with your daughter, go ahead and call it a "date."

You're not babysitting. You can't babysit your own kids. So when your work colleague calls in the middle of your time together, don't say, "I'm babysitting." Say, "I'm on a date with Ashley."

Daughters need to date their dads. If she's a toddler, it's pretty easy. Ten minutes lying in the grass, rustling in the leaves, or making snow angels. If she's five, it's still pretty easy, but invest a half hour. Go for ice cream. McD's. Donuts and juice. A bike ride. Goofing in the driveway with a hula hoop, basketball, bubbles, or sidewalk chalk. By second grade you can teach her four-square or hopscotch. Again, it's just you and her.

Then about third grade or so start thinking about real dates. With a plan, a time, and a destination. A movie date, lunch date, or library date. Take a class together. Coach her sports team. Or sit in the bleachers during her practices and take her out for a Slurpee after. Do something girls do with their moms, like pottery painting, jewelry making, or calligraphy. Go window shopping. Mini golf. Frisbee golf. Visit a museum. Visit a pet store. (Pet a puppy, talk to a parrot, or buy a reptile without mom's permission.) Go ice-skating. Visit an apple orchard. Make a pie. Go horseback riding. Go on a double date with your daughter's best friend and her dad. Go to the bank and start a savings account. Give her $100! Wash Mom's car. Bowling. Bird-watching. Browsing a bookstore. Or just go for a Sunday drive.

In the middle of your date, hope something goes terribly wrong. The bowling alley is overbooked with leagues. The restaurant wait is 90 minutes. The skating rink is closed for repairs. A flat tire. Ants at the picnic. You lock your keys in the car.

With any of these minor catastrophes, you have a delightful opportunity to demonstrate patience, resourcefulness, and a sense of humor. These are all traits your daughter should expect in any fellow who takes her out. Of course, I'm not suggesting you orchestrate any near-calamities on your daddy–daughter dates, but I'm not ruling it out either.

Here's the point. You might think the primary purpose of dating your daughter is quality time for the two of you to make some memories. Nope, sorry. When you take her out, the real reason you need to show up on time, open her car door, treat her with respect, and handle any mishaps with grace and a smile is because you are modeling for your daughter the way any boy should act when she goes out on any date at any time.

Finally, when your daughter does start dating boys her own age, that doesn't mean your dates with her should stop. Actually, that's the season in life when you want to spend more time with her, not less. You may have to work a little harder to get on her busy social calendar. But if you ask nicely, she just might fit you in.

Oh yeah. Dad, don't forget to date your wife too.

―――――――――― **Takeaway** ――――――――――

Daddy–daughter dates don't have to be extravagant. But they do have to be intentional. If it's been more than a couple months since your last dad–daughter rendezvous, go ahead and plan something big for this weekend.

"Watching your daughter being collected by her date feels like handing over a million dollar Stradivarius to a gorilla."

—JIM BISHOP

A Daughter Needs Her Dad...

To Spring for Flowers for the School Bus Driver

I think most elementary schools around the country make a big deal about the one-hundredth day of the school year. It occurs sometime in late January or early February. In our hometown, the kindergarten kids celebrate the day by bringing exactly 100 of something to school for show-and-tell. For some kids that means such uninspired collections as 100 Cheerios glued to a poster board or a zip-lock bag of 100 pennies.

Well, I think dads should inspire their kids to do a little more than that. That's why Max brought 100 helium balloons, Isaac brought 100 balloon animals, and Randy brought a birthday cake with 100 lit candles. (Coincidentally, that year 100-Day happened to fall on Randy's birthday—and, no, the fire alarm didn't go off in the classroom.)

What did Rae Anne bring to 100-Day when she was in kindergarten? One hundred crickets. More accurately, somewhere between 75 and 150 crickets. It's not easy to get an accurate count of crickets inside a shoebox covered with screen. There's lots of jumping and chirping and jumping and chirping. And jumping and chirping. You get the idea.

Rae Anne was very excited about her crickets. The kindergarten teacher not so much. Mrs. Sanders totally appreciated the creativity and extra effort. But she also knew the risk. As a veteran teacher she kept the box of crickets sealed and safe for the entire half-day of class, and she certainly didn't let any of the boys sneak a peek or lift the lid. When the bell finally rang, not a single cricket had escaped the shoebox. Operation 100-Day had been a success! Now all Rae had to do was get the crickets home and turn them loose in a nearby field where they could live free and happy.

Except that's not how it turned out. The actual facts are a bit murky, but here's what we do know. My bride, Rita, was waiting at the corner when the noon kindergarten bus pulled up. The door swung open, and seeing the horrified look on the bus driver's face, Rita had a pretty good idea of what had happened. With encouragement from some of the boys on the bus, Rae Anne had agreed to one more episode of show-and-tell. But somehow the lid came off and it became a surprise episode of jump-and-chirp.

Crickets were everywhere. Girls were screaming. Boys were stomping. Miss Jenny, our wonderful and patient bus driver, was panic-stricken. In a flash, Rae Anne was off the bus, and the bus rolled down the street with a baffled driver, a dozen agitated kids, and a small swarm of unwanted insect passengers.

We're pretty sure there were no formal reports filed. No one got called to the principal's office. But the next morning, Rae Anne did bring a nice bouquet of flowers to Miss Jenny. Strangely enough, that was her last week as bus driver. For the rest of the year, the cricket episode was never mentioned again.

Looking back, no regrets. A girl bringing a box of bugs to school may not be a typical kindergarten scenario. But why settle for typical? Dad, your daughter doesn't always have to be the center of attention, but she should rarely settle for same-o, same-o. Encourage her to approach most assignments, performances, or art projects from a fresh angle. She could write that report on the Jurassic era from the dinosaur's perspective. She could sing "Jingle Bells" while jingling car keys. She could paint a still life with a banana, apple, and worn-out baseball in a wooden bowl.

One more example. Your daughter's sixth-grade science-fair project could very well be something tediously typical like "Which brand of paper towel is most absorbent?" or "Which tastes better—Coke or Pepsi?" Or it could be something entertaining like "Who can pogo-stick the longest, boys or girls?" Then be ready, Dad. If someone breaks an ankle, you may need to spring for another bouquet of flowers.

Takeaway

Sometimes girls just want to blend in. They don't want to be the center of attention. Sometimes they may feel creative and courageous. Dad, you need to know your daughter well in order to read all her signals. Sometimes push her to be daring. Sometimes back off. Try to get it right. But even if you get it wrong, she'll appreciate that you cared enough to be involved.

> *"Of these you may eat any kind of locust, katydid,*
> *cricket or grasshopper. But all other flying insects that*
> *have four legs you are to regard as unclean."*
>
> —LEVITICUS 11:22-23

A Daughter Needs Her Dad…

To Embolden Her to Write Her Own Sticky Notes for Her Own Mirror

Can you say this: "(*Your daughter's name*), those shorts are too short. I can't let you go to school like that"?

Well, a good friend of mine said those exact words to his 13-year-old daughter as she was headed out the door. Her response? She got on the bus and went to school.

Not a fun moment. Actually a very difficult moment. But that dad was saying something that his daughter needed to hear. Something that had to be said.

To be clear, this was not a part-time father who showed up one morning to cast judgment and aspersions on a young teen's fashion choices. This was a dad who had been pouring love, faith, creativity, integrity, and wisdom into his daughter's heart and mind for 13 years. He had talked with her about the value of modesty. He had talked about boys and how they think. He had talked about inner beauty, sexual purity, and setting personal standards.

But he had not talked specifically about the length of blue-jean shorts.

All those earlier conversations ended with a mutual appreciation. He was her greatest fan and she was his. He had listened, delivered biblical truth, told stories from his own youth, and promised to always be there for her. This father and this daughter had always been on the same page. He was protecting her. She was glad about that.

Then suddenly came the morning she headed out the door in shorts that were too short. And he risked it all. This was not a fictional moment far into the future. This was right now, a split-second decision. This was one of those moments of truth that require great courage from a dedicated father.

My friend did not embarrass his daughter in front of a group of her peers. He did not yell. He did not grab her and force her back into the house. He directly spoke truth into her life. And she got on the bus anyway.

Had he failed his daughter? Had he failed God? Can you relate?

The father and daughter did not speak that evening. After a couple of days, their relationship returned to its previous state. Polite dinner-table conversation, coordinating schedules, a clarification about homework, a comment on current events, a laugh over a television show, and a return to the bedtime ritual of prayers and wishes and good-night kisses.

The incident that morning was never mentioned. From the outside looking in, dad and daughter were once again on the same page.

One more thing. She never wore those shorts again. And a sticky note appeared on her full-length bedroom mirror. A note she had written herself. It said, "Does what you see honor God?"

A moment of courage on the part of a dedicated father helps a young teen come to a new understanding of her true value in God's eyes.

Will you have that kind of courage, Dad? Have you earned the right to speak truth into the life of your daughter?

Takeaway

As dads, we need to establish our own beliefs and convictions. We should talk about them and model them with our daughters. But at some point, each of our girls has to own those beliefs and convictions herself. That's going to take courage on your part. And hers.

"I want the men everywhere to pray, lifting up holy hands
without anger or disputing. I also want the women
to dress modestly, with decency and propriety."

—PAUL, IN 1 TIMOTHY 2:8-9

A Daughter Needs Her Dad...
To Get Her a Dog She Can Call Her Own

Madison was our golden retriever. Now think about the timing of her 12-year life span for a moment, especially if you know anything about the gentle, devoted disposition of goldens. We got Madison as a puppy when Rae Anne was three. We put that big old dog to sleep when Rae was 15. Do you think they had a bond? Do you think that Rae Anne insisted—and still does—that Madison was *her* dog? Those two had an undeniable connection.

That dog allowed my daughter to do anything. Rae Anne could watch TV using Madison as a big furry pillow. Rae Anne would line up her stuffed dogs expecting Madison to sit obediently, patiently and motionless in the middle of the polyester collection. And she did.

When Rae Anne was learning to swim, Madison would race around the pool making sure she was safe. The only time Maddie ever jumped on anyone was when they threatened Rae Anne. Sometimes Rae's brothers would pretend to attack their sister just to get the dog riled up.

One story worth telling is the time Madison got skunked. Rae Anne and I washed her with tomato juice, Dawn detergent, and doggy shampoo in our backyard. To see if I had gotten the smell out, I would stick my nose down into her fur. In the process, my beard became skunkified. A clean shave was in order. (For me, not the dog.) As a result, 13-year-old Rae Anne saw me without my beard for the first time in her life.

Two other dogs overlapped our life with Madison. Both were much smaller and didn't shed near as much. Neither would be considered Rae

Anne's. Cubby was our first dog, a mutt from a shelter that I guess we might call "Randy's Dog." Actually, we got Madison because it was clear that Cubby was slowing way down and didn't have much time left. Wouldn't you know it, introducing a golden retriever puppy to a 15-year-old mutt perked up the old guy. We had two dogs for two years. I do remember that Cubby did not much appreciate Madison's comical attempts as a newly weaned puppy to find a place to nurse from him.

Briggs, an energetic silky terrier who only bit the mail carrier once, is still with us and her story continues to be written. For Rae Anne, of course, no dog could replace her Maddie.

Should every little girl get a dog? Probably not. But if you've got a yard and a little girl who's fascinated by dogs, I totally recommend it. Rae Anne made Madison a better dog. And Madison had a profound effect on my daughter. Love is a powerful force in any form it takes.

When it was time to put her down, I gave Rae Anne the option of waiting outside while the vet did her work. But I knew what my daughter would do. She and I sat on the floor of the vet's examining room and stroked her dog gently and thanked her for being part of our family and giving us a real-life example of unconditional love.

Every member of our family will always have an appreciation for any golden retriever we see out for a walk with its master. But what I can't get over is that—with that breed—about one out of ten dogs will look exactly, and I mean exactly, like Madison. Almost a decade later, it still startles me and almost takes my breath away. Silly, huh?

Takeaway

The day you bring that puppy home, take lots of photos of your new family member with your daughter. They grow so fast. The dog does too.

*"No symphony orchestra ever played music like a
two-year-old girl laughing with a puppy."*

—Bern Williams

A Daughter Needs Her Dad…

To Write Her Name on the Moon

Because there is no atmosphere on the moon, boot prints left by astronauts remain undisturbed. Essentially forever. There's no wind, rain, or life to scatter the dust. Which also means the initials "TDC" are still scrawled in the moondust about a mile from the landing site of the Apollo 17 lunar module.

Before leaving on his 1972 lunar odyssey, Commander Eugene Cernan had promised his nine-year-old daughter that he was going to bring her "back a moonbeam." At least that's what Tracy Cernan said during an interview on *The Today Show* while her daddy explored, conducted scientific experiments, and frolicked some 239,000 miles from home. Well, moonbeams are hard to capture and don't last anyway. So Captain Cernan, who would be the last man to walk on the moon, did the next best thing. After spending 75 hours on the lunar surface, his last official assignment was to drive the four-wheeled lunar rover some distance away from the lunar module and adjust the vehicle's camera to transmit video of the launch later that day. Before loping back to the lunar module, that father bent down and traced his daughter's initials in the dust, giving Teresa Dawn Cernan a monument unlike any other girl on any other planet.

Pretty cool, huh?

Well, I totally recommend all dads do the exact same thing next time you're on the moon. But if that's not on your calendar this year, let's consider how Captain Cernan's tracings in honor of his daughter may be replicated here on earth.

Quite literally, you could leave your daughter's initials in a variety of creative locations. If you happen to be pouring a foundation for a patio or other new construction, you could certainly draw a heart containing her initials in the wet cement. On a fencepost in the corner of your yard or a tree stump at the family cottage, you could carve a subtle tribute. You could have her initials inscribed on a coin or key chain you carry in your pocket. Or on a letter opener or some other office accessory. It's not my style, but some readers may consider sitting for a tattoo of your daughter's name or initials. Tastefully rendered, of course.

Initials on the moon are especially sentimental because they are unique, permanent, and intentional. Even though Cernan's gesture was made public, the connection between the astronaut and his daughter is quite private. He knows it. She knows it. And it's part of a father-to-daughter legacy set in stone.

Beyond creative engravings of her name or initials, there are other ways to memorialize your love for your daughter. Dedicate something to her that has artistic, architectural, educational, poetic, or literary value. Be creative. More than one housing developer has snuck a Rachel Avenue or Lindsay Boulevard into a new neighborhood. *Carly* or *Amelia* is certainly a better name for your yacht than *Seas the Day* or *Breakin' Wind*. Dave Thomas named his fast-food restaurant chain after his daughter Wendy. In 1949, bakery entrepreneur Charlie Lubin named his cheesecake after his eight-year-old daughter, Sara Lee. An Austrian businessman, one of the first customers of automotive pioneers Gottlieb Daimler and Karl Benz, placed an order for 36 custom-designed cars, insisting they be named for his daughter Mercedes.

In the course of your job, hobby, or vacation experience is there someplace you can interpose an icon or image of your daughter? It might simply be a smiling photo on your screensaver, bulletin board, or dashboard.

Dad, I know you think of your daughter often. Hundreds of times per day. You pause, picture her beautiful face, and pray for her well-being. But she doesn't know that. The real reason to make an obvious and clear statement that she means the sun, moon, and stars to you is not to remind you. It's to remind her.

Takeaway

A few pages into this book, you'll see my dedication to Rae Anne, so I'm already heading down the right path in this area. Guys, I dare you to beat that.

> *"I thank my God every time I remember you. In all my prayers for all of you, I always pray with joy because of your partnership in the gospel from the first day until now, being confident of this, that he who began a good work in you will carry it on to completion until the day of Christ Jesus."*
>
> —Philippians 1:3-6

A Daughter Needs Her Dad...

To Not Comment on Every Little Thing

Dad, when it comes to your daughter, be smart enough to know that you should not comment on every little thing. And by that I mean some of the big things.

There are big things in your daughter's life that you know about and she knows about, but you need to pretend that you don't know about.

Let me restate that. Shut up about personal stuff.

At the risk of totally embarrassing myself, my daughter, you, and your daughter, I am about to list a few of those things. In advance of that, I apologize. Let's just consider this a public service for all dads who are trying to prove how hip they are by talking about stuff that they really shouldn't be talking about. Yes, Dad, you should be involved in your daughter's life. You should have wonderful, deep conversations about her pursuit of excellence and God's plan for her life. Go ahead and ask her questions that give you insight into her hopes, dreams, fears, and frustrations. Be available. Be huggable. Don't be intimidated or afraid of talking with your daughter.

You can talk about the traits she should look for in a boy worth dating. You can talk about the poor choices made by fictional characters on television shows you watch together. You can even talk about fashion. Specifically how modesty is usually the best choice and how boys can look at what a girl is wearing and get the wrong impression very quickly.

But again, let me repeat. There are some things you should not be talking about. Frankly, I should not even be typing them out. Nevertheless, here they are: Puberty. Menstruation. Facial hair. Body hair. Acne. Body odor. Cramps. PMS. Bathroom scales. Bras. Feminine hygiene products. Gynecological exams. Her first crush. Her first kiss. Her first broken heart.

If she comes to you and opens the door on any of these topics, choose your words carefully and listen more than talk. But don't expect such a conversation to take place. That's what moms are for.

Which leads us to a brief segue paying homage to all the courageous single dads out there who are raising a daughter without a mom or step-mom in the home. All those sensitive issues mentioned above can't be ignored by single dads. You'll need to be able to talk about them in the most basic of terms. Still, you're going to want to recruit some assistance. The recommended course of action is to enlist the help of a woman you trust to answer any question your daughter might have. An aunt, older cousin, doctor, neighbor who happens to be a nurse, pastor's wife, or family friend. Humbly admit that you can't do that part of parenting alone. Then get your daughter involved in choosing that over-21 mentor with whom she will be comfortable. Find someone who does more than just answer specific questions, but also anticipates other physical, emotional, and spiritual challenges your daughter will be facing.

In most cases, dads should expect to be kept on a need-to-know basis. If you're called upon to make a late-night run to the drugstore, keep your mouth shut and do it. If your daughter suddenly gets weepy about some boy you barely know, trust your wife to dry the tears. Later, she'll fill in any details you need to know. Or not.

Frankly, Dad, this is all good news. Your wife and daughter aren't keeping you out of the loop. They're not denying your importance. They're simply protecting you from stuff you can't help with anyway. And they're saving you for those life challenges that require the big guns, manly decisions, and your powerful presence. You'll know when you're needed.

Takeaway

It's good to be a guy.

"Think what cowards men would be if they had to bear children. Women are an altogether superior species."
—George Bernard Shaw

A Daughter Needs Her Dad…

To Treat Her the Same as a Boy 78 Percent of the Time

think I need to respectfully disagree with any militant feminists out there who claim the only reason girls are different from boys is gender stereotyping and environmental influences.

My position is this: Girls need unconditional love, encouragement, instruction, physical challenges, time with dad, chores, discipline, respect, a sense of right and wrong, a relationship with God, hugs, sleep, birthday parties, bike rides, chocolate-chip cookies, trees to climb, and all kinds of opportunities to explore their world and find their place in it. Boys need all the same stuff.

As a matter of fact, my first bestselling book, *52 Things Kids Need from a Dad*, spent 50 chapters lumping all kids in the same pot. Dad, no matter what their gender, you have to be intentional about pouring your love, commitment, and compassion into their little hearts from the day they're conceived until the day you die.

That challenge is going to take a mighty dose of your time, energy, and creativity, Dad. Because, you see, no two kids are alike. Let me repeat: *No two kids are alike.* Let me also repeat that one of your most important jobs, Dad, is to help every child you may have to reach the highest potential following the purpose and path God has planned for him or her. If you haven't yet picked up that theme in this book, you haven't really been paying attention.

But back to your daughter. Anyone without some kind of agenda who has actually spent time observing children over the years will agree that obvious differences between boys and girls show up at a very young age. And I'm not talking about different private parts and diaper-changing techniques. Or dressing them in pinks and blues.

Baby girls watch you more closely. Girls talk sooner. Girls have larger vocabularies and longer attention spans. Girls use words as tools and weapons, hence the idea of "feminine wiles." Boys are more physically aggressive—more likely to grab, push, wrestle, and throw things. Girls relate. Boys explore. As one of my close friends describes it, "Girls need nose-to-nose time with Dad and boys need shoulder-to-shoulder time."

Now since every child is different, there are some "boy" traits that show up in girls. And vice versa. Some boys do talk earlier than their sisters. Some girls are natural explorers or more competitive than the boy down the street. Mass generalizations give guidance, not absolute direction.

But here's what ticks me off. It seems like every study done in the last half-century has set out to prove the opposite of what is true. Researchers with an agenda decide ahead of time what outcome they want and then attempt to justify their prejudice. A supposedly groundbreaking study was published in the September 2005 issue of *American Psychologist* magazine. The title of the article, by Professor Janet Shibley Hyde of the University of Wisconsin–Madison, is "The Gender Similarities Hypothesis." The 12-page article, which includes two pages of references, several charts and graphs, and lots of big words, is quite impressive. Dr. Hyde looks at a wide variety of personality and cognitive traits, including memory, self-esteem, social behavior, communication, small motor skills, negotiation, smiling, coping, delayed gratification, cheating, assertiveness, and anxiety just to name a few. Her conclusion is that 46 meta-analyses confirm that men and women are unequivocally and undeniably very much alike. But buried deep in the article is this statement: "78 percent of gender differences are small or close to zero."[1]

Did you get that? Boys and girls are *not* the same. Seventy-eight percent of the time they are. But after compiling research from more than 2000 studies, science finally agrees that in 22 percent of the categories, *men and women are significantly different.* Shouldn't that have been the title of the article?

Reviewing the media coverage that followed this 2005 report, the consensus seemed to be that there is zero difference between boys and girls, and parents should be ashamed for treating them differently. Well, science says otherwise.

So, good news, Dad, the book you're holding is valid. There are unique strategies and guidelines you need to consider when raising your daughter. I'm oversimplifying, but 78 percent of the time your interaction with a daughter will be the same as the interaction with a son. They will delight in piggyback rides, ice-cream cones, and first-place trophies. They will be sad when they are cut from a team, are punished for disobedience, or get a rejection letter from a college. But the other 22 percent of time, a daughter will be different from a son.

Your job, Dad, is to become a student of your daughter and bask in the challenge of discovering and guiding her toward her own very individual hopes and dreams.

Takeaway

Open doors for your daughter. Be the dad who provides her with many wonderful and exciting opportunities. Include "girl" things and "boy" things. In the end, make sure that what she ends up pouring her time and effort into are "her" things and not "your" things. Okay?

> *"God created mankind in his own image,*
> *in the image of God he created them;*
> *male and female he created them."*
>
> —GENESIS 1:27

A Daughter Needs Her Dad...
To Not Panic About Her Decrees

During the years your daughter is living under your roof, she may make one or more unexpected pronouncements. Often at the dinner table. Occasionally out of the blue during a commercial break when you're all watching your favorite TV show. Perhaps that decree will be launched with no advance warning from the backseat of the SUV on a family outing. Or maybe while you're tucking her in after a good day or bad day or day of mixed emotions.

Every girl at every age is different, but her pronouncements may include statements like these:

"I'm going to marry Justin Bieber."

"I'm never getting married."

"I'm going to be a veterinarian when I grow up."

"I'm going to be an advice columnist when I grow up."

"I'm majoring in economics, then going to law school, and then into politics to finally fix the U.S. economy."

"Aubrey and I are getting our tongues pierced."

"I'm running for student council."

"The track team doesn't have a pole-vaulter, so I volunteered."

"I'm painting my bedroom magenta."

"I'm moving to the attic."

"I'm moving in with Scott."

"Until farmers stop using milking machines, I'm going to boycott all dairy products."

"I'm getting out at the next stoplight and hitchhiking home."

The list could go on. And as outlandish as some of these declarations might be, I'm guessing your daughter has or will pull out some doozies of her own that are even more surprising. Maybe she's testing you. Maybe she's absolutely sincere. Maybe she's confused and has no idea what she's saying.

These pronouncements will evoke emotional reactions. However, Dad, I urge you to take a breath. Do not overreact. Do not panic. Do not speak the words you initially want to speak. Most of your gut responses would not open the door to dialogue. (And dialogue is the goal of the moment.)

Because we're caught off guard, most of us dads immediately respond with our own declarative statement. Something like...

"That's awesome. Go for it."

"That's ridiculous."

"I wouldn't count on it, if I were you."

"Over my dead body."

"No. That is not your decision to make."

While these responses are not necessarily wrong, Dad, you can see how they may very well cause your daughter to either clam up or go ballistic.

A preferable fatherly response to just about any of her surprising declarations is something like "Really? Tell me what went into your making that decision." It's okay if your tone of voice reveals your opinion. But your initial goal is simply to persuade her to share the thought process leading up to her decree. Hopefully she will share two or three more sentences that uncover the catalyst for her bold decision.

No matter how you feel about her initial declaration, you really do want to gather information. To open the floor for conversation. To pave a smooth avenue down which you can eventually deliver your profound input based on years of experience, undeniable wisdom, and caring perspective. Even more important, you'll want this conversation to be the first of many on this topic, if necessary. That way you will have the opportunity to seek out your own wise counsel, study Scripture, talk to your daughter's mom, and perhaps even do some extensive research into an area in which you have zero expertise.

Of course, consider the source and the tone. If the declaration came from a precocious three-year-old, count your blessings and consider it good practice. But if it's a life-altering pronouncement from the little girl you've known for 18 years, you'll want to be ready with a receptive attitude and some open-ended questions that allow you to know what's really at the root of the matter.

Practice it now, Dad. "Really? Tell me what went into your making that decision." Seriously, say it out loud. Slowly. A couple times. Try saying it with a hint of judgment. Or with a hint of delight. Try saying it as if you are truly surprised and curious about her thinking process.

Isn't it nice to have your response prepared before you need to respond? It happens so rarely to dads of daughters.

Takeaway

When your daughter hits you with a surprising declaration, she already has an idea of how she thinks you will respond. Surprise her right back with your own version of the line, "Really! How did you come to make that decision?"

"My dear brothers and sisters, take note of this: Everyone should be quick to listen, slow to speak and slow to become angry, because human anger does not produce the righteousness that God desires."

JAMES 1:19-20

A Daughter Needs Her Dad…

To Raise Her as a Princess Among Knaves

I wish you could have attended Rae Anne's first birthday. The professionally printed invitation featured a pink and purple castle and an eight-line poem written by her daddy specifically for the occasion.

> *Hear Ye! Hear Ye!*
> *All knaves, serfs and vassals.*
> *Thou art commanded to come*
> *To the Princess' castle.*
>
> *Her birthday mark one*
> *Has arrived as you've dreaded.*
> *Choose not to attend*
> *And thou shalt be beheaded.*

Knaves Alec, Randy, Max, and Isaac wore burlap vests cinched with twine. Rae Anne wore a pink princess frock with a simple yet elegant tiara. Using my finest carpentry skills and set-designing techniques learned in college theater classes, I fashioned a pink brick castle and moat on our front porch, complete with working drawbridge. When guests arrived, the drawbridge would be lowered with much fanfare and silliness. Of course, my only daughter remembers none of this. But it was all captured in photos and video. If I can find them, I should probably do some video editing and YouTube posting.

But the point is, your little girl will always be part princess. Even when she's smashing birthday cake into her high chair, climbing the gnarly oak tree in the neighbor's yard, or attempting to clear nine feet on the pole vault. When you look at her—close up or from a distance—she will always, always, always be part princess.

Especially if she has brothers, don't be afraid to treat her a little differently. Because she is different!

All this talk about princesses should come with a word of warning. While you do want to treat your daughter like a princess, you don't want to raise a princess. There is a difference. From father to daughter, you want her to feel like the most beautiful and precious girl in the world. So special that she realizes early on that she has a wide range of unique gifts and powers. So competent that she does not need to depend on others for her personal fulfillment. She's not entitled, but empowered. She's not selfish, but self-reliant. She'll never be a victim because she has the power to choose to walk away from abuse or fight for justice.

One example of how this plays out is your daughter's choice of husband. If you raise a princess, she may end up with the first guy who indulges her ego. But if you imbue her with ambition and sound judgment, she'll save herself for one man who is worthy of her affections.

In her well-researched book *Strong Fathers, Strong Daughters*, Meg Meeker, MD, challenges us men to raise our daughters not as princesses but as pioneer women. In chapter 6, "Pragmatism and Grit," Dr. Meeker writes,

> Princesses take. Princesses want more. Princesses demand. They expect perfection and lack pragmatism. They don't act—except to tell others what they want. But pioneer women know that life is the way it is, and they rely on themselves to move forward...Inevitably, your daughter will encounter pain. People die and loved ones get cancer. She might not get asked to the prom. She might get pregnant at sixteen. She might develop an eating disorder. She will encounter problems, like you did. Some can be solved, some cannot. But if she is to live a substantive, healthy life, she needs to decide what to do about her problems...When princesses get bad grades, or get pregnant at sixteen, or get kicked out of school, it's always because someone else messed up; it's always someone else's fault.[2]

If I can summarize: Pioneer women take responsibility. Princesses just take.

I don't think Dr. Meeker would fault my wife and me for throwing a "princess party" for Rae Anne's first birthday. Frankly, more than just about any young woman I know, Rae Anne has the can-do pioneer spirit that will serve her well wherever her dreams and God's calling take her.

And those knavish brothers? They will always be her greatest cheerleaders.

Takeaway

How about a compromise? Raise your daughter as a princess with grit. Or a pioneer woman with grace. No matter what, don't forget to throw her a fantastical first birthday party. Even if she is your fifth kid!

"To the outside world we all grow old. But not to brothers and sisters.
We know each other as we always were. We know each other's hearts.
We share private family jokes. We remember family feuds and
secrets, family griefs and joys. We live outside the touch of time."

—Clara Ortega

A Daughter Needs Her Dad…

To Willingly Do the Hokey Pokey, the Macarena, and Even the Chicken Dance

Sometimes you just have to surrender, put on your dancing shoes, and boogie. That's right—once a year or so it's your fatherly responsibility to make a complete fool of yourself in a public place along with dozens of other dads and daughters. I'm talking, of course, about the "Daddy–Daughter Date Nite" that takes place each year at park districts, schools, community centers, country clubs, and even churches around the country.

For the uninitiated, here's what you can expect. The events are just dads (and maybe some granddads or uncles) and their daughters up to about fifth grade. No moms or brothers allowed. The dads wear anything from nice shirts and slacks to tuxedos. The young ladies are dressed in their finest party dresses, hair done just so, and wearing all the jewelry they might own. When she was about five, Rae Anne insisted on wearing a princess tiara she had somehow acquired and that was just fine with me. After I had raised four court jesters, she was indeed my princess.

You can be as formal and chivalrous as you want, but do consider ringing your own doorbell, pinning on a corsage, posing for pictures, helping with her coat, opening car doors, and just being generally gallant. The event probably does not include dinner, but will have snacks and beverages. Bonus activities may include a magician or clown, balloon animals, complimentary photos, and party favors.

The highlight of the event is the dance itself, 90 minutes of songs you know and love that will have you and your daughter or daughters singing along and shaking your booties. Every town seems to have a DJ who specializes in daddy–daughter events, and he knows how to get the crowd moving. The younger girls playfully swing on their daddy's arm or race around the floor. But the older girls—not quite young women—have a certain unspoken wistfulness about them, as they know that childhood is coming to an end. The dads know that too. Often this will be the last time they dance together until her wedding reception more than a decade away.

I can't think about "Daddy–Daughter Date Nite" without giving a nod to Terry and Ally Schweizer, who served as double-date partners for Rae Anne and me for several of these annual events. Each year, Terry would pick us up, and invariably the girls would sit in the backseat comparing their jewelry and outfits. The double date worked out well because both Ally and Rae Anne have four brothers, and one-on-one time with dad is highly coveted.

One key bit of advice for the evening is to stick with your date. At grown-up dinner parties with your wife, sometimes the women congregate in one area and the men circle up in another. But this is a rare daddy–daughter event—you can catch up with the other dads some other time. Also, I suggest you mentally prepare yourself to surrender to the instructions of the DJ. Even if you're the kind of guy who just doesn't dance, getting out on the floor is an essential part of the evening. The worst thing that happens is that you give your daughter something to tease you about. So, if you are instructed to put your right hip in and shake it all about, just do it. If a human locomotive chugs by, grab on. And please don't forget how to spell Y-M-C-A.

The evening will go by quickly. And so will the years. Pretty soon she'll be in middle school, way too mature for the organized "Daddy–Daughter Date Nite." When that inevitable transformation occurs, I recommend you create a revised, scaled-down version of the event for just you and your blossoming daughter. When the park district brochure comes out, let the announcement serve as a reminder to do a new enhanced kind of Daddy–Daughter Date. Make reservations for two at one of the nicer restaurants in town. Instead of doing the hokey pokey, maybe the two of you can sit by candlelight and just talk. Talk about what's going on in her life. About girlfriends, hobbies, hopes and dreams. About boys and silly stuff that brothers and moms just don't get.[3]

Takeaway

Check with your local park district or ask some other dads you know about the nearest "Daddy–Daughter Date Nite." Put it on your calendar. Surrender yourself to the evening. Make it magical. If your little girl is not so little anymore, do your own daddy–daughter date night anyway.

> *"The father of a daughter is nothing but a high-class hostage. A father turns a stony face to his sons, berates them, shakes his antlers, paws the ground, snorts, runs them off into the underbrush, but when his daughter puts her arm over his shoulder and says, 'Daddy, I need to ask you something,' he is a pat of butter in a hot frying pan."*
>
> —GARRISON KEILLOR

A Daughter Needs Her Dad…

To Let Her Aspire to Be a Housewife

Let me be clear. I am not saying you should program your daughter to be "just a housewife." Or insist that she become a "homemaker." Or "stay-at-home mom." Or a "domestic engineer."

What I am saying is this. Your little girl will very likely go through a season of life in which she envisions herself as a mommy. When that happens, by all means nurture that vocation. Aspiring to be a mom should be a part of every little girl's growing-up dreams. Does that sound sexist? It's not. It's all about honoring the role of motherhood and the many rewarding possibilities it brings. It's all about recognizing the wonderful soul-satisfying role that no man will ever fully understand. Carrying a child. Giving birth. Breast-feeding. Nurturing a toddler. Giving a "mom" hug as only a mom can.

Dads, it's okay to be slightly jealous of the gifts and capabilities of the female of our species. But only a little. We have our own cool aptitudes and responsibilities. And there's lots of overlap these days in what once were traditionally male and female roles. Yea for dads who do mommy stuff. Yea for moms who do daddy stuff. Still, despite some pro-mommy movements, homemakers continue to lose ground culturally, socially, and politically. Women who choose motherhood as their primary focus while their children are in their formative years aren't getting the respect they deserve.

There seems to be a branch of feminism that has proclaimed war on motherhood. They downplay and diminish the role of mothers in our culture. These women—and some men—assert that nurturing a child from conception to independence is a mundane, thankless existence. They insist any parent that allows their daughter to play with dolls is stunting her potential. These so-called advocates for feminine empowerment shriek that it's a waste for any thinking woman to push a stroller through a park, call her family to dinner, or volunteer at school.

This short chapter is not going to sway the thinking of any radical feminists. But I hope it does serve as a reminder to a few dads that your brilliant, beautiful, talented daughter may choose to spend much of her twenties, thirties, and forties answering the honorable call of raising a family. And that's a great thing.

A few rhetorical questions will cement that thinking. "When your three-year-old daughter picks up a doll and begins to rock it in her arms, should you slap that doll away onto the floor?" "When your high-school freshman looks up from her novel and says the name of the hero would be a great name for a baby, should you chastise her for thinking such ridiculous thoughts?" "As you walk your 23-year-old daughter down the aisle on her wedding day, should you whisper a warning not to make any babies until her college loan is paid off and remind her that she'd better make good use of her expensive degree in marketing?"

Dad, when your little girl rocks dolls, dreams about baby names, and gets married, those are all signs that you and your daughter's mother are doing something right. She sees building a family as a worthy goal.

When radical feminists trash-talk stay-at-home moms, I'm convinced they may be revealing their own regrets and even some jealousy. The choices and societal pressures facing the next generation of moms (including your daughter) will require much prayer and prioritizing.

Do you want your little girl to reach her full potential? Of course. Do you want her to give you grandchildren to brag about and spoil? Of course. Is it okay if she chooses to make raising those children her first priority for a season of life? Dad, you need to make sure she feels good about that decision.

Takeaway

Dad, if your daughter or daughter-in-law chooses to stay in the workforce during her children's formative years, it's vital that you don't lay on layers of guilt. A better response might be to consider what you can do to be a helpful resource for your adult children, enter the lives of your grandchildren, and fill in the gaps.

> *"I think I can understand that feeling about a housewife's work being like that of Sisyphus (who was the stone rolling gentleman). But it is surely, in reality, the most important work in the world. What do ships, railways, mines, cars, government, etc. exist for except that people may be fed, warmed, and safe in their own homes?... We wage war in order to have peace, we work in order to have leisure, we produce food in order to eat it. So your job is the one for which all others exist."*
>
> —C.S. Lewis

A Daughter Needs Her Dad…

To Remember That Less Is More

My little sister, Sue, tells this story about my dad from a couple decades ago.

She was just 21 and living at home. This was before cell phones. She rolled into our gravel driveway about 2:30 a.m. Dad met her at the front screen door in his sleep attire—pretty much a T-shirt and gym shorts. Sue would later describe his face as ashen. Stepping onto the front porch, she set her jaw, prepared for a verbal assault of some kind. Maybe leading to a heated argument with words that both father and daughter would regret later. But for whatever reason, Dad didn't go there. He just said what needed to be said: "All you had to do was call." Then he turned and finally, with a little brokenness, went to bed for the night.

As a current dad and former young person, you know the impact of those seven words. My sister affirms that my father's statement—true, concise, and convicting—had a greater impact on her life than any half-hour rant, 50-foot banner, or PowerPoint presentation detailing reasons to respect your parents.

And that's why this chapter is so short. Sometimes—often—less is more.

Takeaway

Think before you speak. When you deliver an ultimatum, be prepared for the worst-case scenario. Don't try to outsmart, outthink, or outargue your daughter. Whoever screams first, loses. Instead, use quiet words, create quiet connections, and make quiet requests. Phrases like "I need your help" or "I miss you," have much more impact than "You are in so much trouble" or "That's a ridiculous idea."

> *"Never fear big long words.*
> *Big long words name little things.*
> *All big things have little names.*
> *Such as life and death, peace and war.*
> *Or dawn, day, night, hope, love, home.*
> *Learn to use little words in a big way.*
> *It is hard to do,*
> *But they say what you mean.*
> *When you don't know what you mean, use big words.*
> *That often fools little people."*
>
> —ARTHUR KUDNER

A Daughter Needs Her Dad...

To Totally Embarrass Her Once in a While

Once a month or so, you want your daughter to think or even say, "Dad, you're embarrassing me." That's a sign you're doing something right.

For one thing, it means you're spending some quantity time with your daughter and her friends. That's an important litmus test for the father–daughter relationship. If you don't know her friends, if they don't feel welcome at your home, then you need to work on that. Make your home a hangout. Keep soda in the fridge and chips in the cabinet. Establish a comfort zone in your home that's inviting to her peers, with just enough privacy that they feel like they can talk, laugh, share secrets, and make life-long connections. You need to be able to enter or pass through that space without too much of an apology. If you have a bag of Dilly Bars or a bowl of popcorn, that makes it even easier.

Also, embarrassing your daughter in front of her friends proves that she cares about what you do and who you are. Here are a few methods that pretty much guarantee an eye roll, major blush, and pleading outburst from your school-age daughter. Lip-syncing to songs playing on her iPod. Singing right along to songs playing on her iPod. Dancing of any kind. Pulling out her baby pictures. Using her secret name from when she was a toddler, like "Woobie" or "Lolly." Wearing socks that cover your calves while you have shorts on. Kissing your wife in the kitchen. Attempting and failing to use text lingo. Asking her girlfriends if they have boyfriends.

The lighthearted act of embarrassing your daughter turns serious as she moves through her teens. Embarrassing questions may need to be asked: "Where are you going?" "What movie are you seeing?" "Who else is going?" "Can I give you twenty bucks for cab fare if you need it?" "Got your cell phone?" "You know you can call me anytime and I'll be there. For you or your friends."

My recommendation is to let these questions come out of your mouth while her friends are within earshot. As the group heads out the door or down the driveway, you actually do want her to roll her eyes and say to her girlfriends, "My dad worries about me way too much." Some of the girls will say, "So does my dad." Others will stay silent, wishing their father would say those things. Or maybe wishing they had a father.

Even more powerful is saying these things in front of a young man who may or may not be attempting to seduce your daughter. Your words have effectively given that lecherous little creep one more reason to keep his hands to himself. He will receive the message that this girl has a dad who cares. And he won't be surprised when she sets some dating standards. By the way, that young man may also be in need of a father figure who isn't afraid to ask a couple basic questions. It all adds up.

But it all begins with your daughter's girlfriends and boyfriends feeling welcome in your home. So you need to know when to be slightly embarrassing and when to be cool. When to enter their world. And when to trust that you've done enough.

Later that night, when she comes home from her teenage adventures, your earlier questions have given you accurate information to launch an adult conversation. "How was the movie?" "How was that new restaurant?" "Did Kyle pay or did you go dutch?" "Can I have my twenty bucks back?"

Takeaway

Of course, the goal is not really to embarrass your daughter. The goal is to stay connected to who she is becoming and what's going on in her life. It's a natural progression that eventually will come full circle. Embarrassing young people slightly with your "old-fashioned" perspective is a much better choice than dressing like them, talking like them, and trying to still be a teen yourself. Now that's embarrassing.

> *"To an adolescent, there is nothing in the world*
> *more embarrassing than a parent."*
>
> —DAVE BARRY

A Daughter Needs Her Dad…

To Enter Her in an
Ice-Cream-Eating Contest

If you enter your preschool daughter in an ice-cream-eating contest, you probably shouldn't expect her to win. But I pretty much knew Rae Anne would.

It was the annual Pride of the Fox RiverFest. Eight 4- and 5-year-olds were seated at the long tables facing the crowds in the parking lot of Colonial Ice Cream. Having watched her four older brothers in hundreds of sporting events and heated brother battles, Rae Anne understood the idea of competing with determination and excellence. We had taught her to use a spoon when she ate ice cream, but she also knew that sometimes desperate times called for desperate measures.

To most of those in the crowd—and probably the other seven contestants—this was clearly a trivial and inconsequential precursor to the upcoming rounds featuring more serious ice-cream eating by school-age kids, teenagers, and adults. Rae Anne did not feel that way. If it's a competition, she knows you compete to win. If the spoon slows you down, dig in with your hands. If the goal is to empty the pint of ice cream first, it's perfectly acceptable to finish with a certain percentage of ice cream on your face. When the cheers get louder, eat faster. When you are declared the winner, raise your arms in victory.

The newspaper photographer captured it all. The photos were so awesome that they were featured on the cover of the Pride of the Fox booklet the following year. And you can check them out on jaypayleitner.com, my website.

This all took place in 1997 in St. Charles, Illinois. It's the town where I met, courted, and married my high-school sweetheart...and the home of Colonial Ice Cream, the annual Pride of the Fox RiverFest, the annual Scarecrow Festival, two paddle-wheel riverboats, Christmas walks, farmer's markets, art shows, the nationally recognized Kane County Flea Market, parades, fireworks, theater guilds, choral groups, a concert band, bike trails, skate parks, splash pools, a charming downtown, and history galore. The schools are top-notch. The churches are vibrant. High-school sports are big. Devotion to family is even bigger. We mow lawns in summer, rake leaves in fall, and shovel snow in winter. We lock our doors at night, but we still welcome and wave to strangers.

We're not Mayberry (and don't want to be), but last year we were chosen by *Family Circle* magazine as the number-one place in the country to raise a family. That's first place. The same as Rae Anne got in her ice-cream-eating contest.

I tell you all this for three reasons. One, the story from 1997 is fun to tell. Rae Anne was awesome that day. And still is.

Two, I'm proud of my town. I've had a few chances to take a job in another state, but I just couldn't move my family away from their hometown and extended family. Worth noting, my wife, Rita, poured her heart into volunteering at the St. Charles public schools for 20 years and was so appreciated that when our fifth kid graduated, Rita was asked to run for city alderman...and won.

And three, Dad, for that season of life in which your daughter is putting down roots you will want to give her a great community to call her own. Surround her with awesome neighbors and wonderful opportunities to try new things in a safe, creative, and nurturing environment. Invest in the community yourself—not money, but share your talents, experience, and passions. Establish a solid cultural, spiritual, civic, and educational foundation from which she can launch herself into life. This is so important that you should be willing to re-evaluate and even sacrifice your own short-term career goals for her security and well-being.

By the way. I'm not inviting you to move to St. Charles, because 35,000 people is the right-size town for us. That is, unless you're really cool and want to join my men's small group.

Takeaway

To be honest, my hometown works for me and my family. You need to find the right place for your family. You may live in the middle of a prairie with the nearest neighbor ten miles away or in a fourth-floor walk-up on the upper west side of Manhattan. You may be living in the house your grampa was born in. Or you may move every year because of military or job requirements. No matter what, you need to give your little girl a firm foundation that she calls home.

"When you finally go back to your old hometown, you find
it wasn't the home you missed but your childhood."

—SAM EWING

A Daughter Needs Her Dad...

To Dance in and out of Her World

It's easy to enter the world of your four-year-old daughter. All a daddy has to do is say, "Hey, sweetie, what's up?" Or even easier, "Wanna read a book?" Promise her a dash of your attention, and your little girl will drop everything to spend time with you.

That all changes somewhere in middle school. A 12-year-old girl still wants to spend time with her father. But she's also setting up boundaries, building protective walls, and trying to figure out how to make her own decisions. That's part of becoming a young woman. By that age, she has already been burned by some relationships—snubbed by a good friend, taken advantage of by a classmate, or belittled by someone she trusted. (Maybe you, Dad.)

Suddenly, the idea of entering your daughter's world becomes a little trickier. You need to make it happen, but you need to use all your cunning and resourcefulness. That off-limits space might be her bedroom, classroom, practice field, youth center at church, or just a forbidden zone she has created by sitting at your dining-room table with headphones plugged into her laptop. Yes, she's your daughter and you're in charge, but you need a reason to interrupt her self-absorbed world.

Following are a few possible strategic methods for interrupting her privacy without seeming like an interruption.

Give yourself a mutual mission. Asking a young person's opinion is surprising and empowering. *"For Christmas, should I get Mom the amethyst* *or opal earrings?" "What should we do for Grampa's birthday this year?" "We need some new patio chairs. What are your thoughts?"*

Treat her as an authority. Suddenly, she's the teacher and you're the student. *"Hey, Sara, can I send a photo on my iPhone that's 1.8 megabytes?" "I'm designing a flyer for the block party, can you take a look at this font?" "Bill from work wants me to recommend some summer reading for his daughter who's eight. Any ideas?"*

Volunteer at an event. Initially, she may not be happy that you signed up for that chaperone assignment, church event, or fund-raiser. But if you don't embarrass her and stay in your assigned zone, she'll be glad you're there. Also, make sure you give her plenty of notice. *"The Zimmermans asked us to help out at the Christmas dance. I guess we're in charge of the punch bowl." "Just letting you know, I'm driving one of the vans for the weekend retreat. And I'm staying in the boys' cabin."*

Get her attention. Figure out what middle-school girls like—specifically your daughter and her friends—and give it to her. *"Let's get a puppy." "Don't know what got into me, but I bought a Groupon for horseback riding." "When that movie comes out from that book you read, let's take some of your friends to the midnight show." "Pizza's here!"*

Tell her you miss her. If you haven't had a good conversation in a couple weeks, you're both feeling the same way. *"Hey, kiddo. We have both been so busy, let's do something this weekend. Maybe brunch after church. Or we could go to the flea market. What's your schedule?" "You know, I'm reading a book for dads of daughters and it says I'm supposed to ask you out on a date. So pick a night. Any night!"*

For a few years, expect your daughter to retreat just a little from the family. It may be the same season that she stops sitting on your lap. Don't assume it's permanent. Don't assume you've done something wrong. My advice is that when she steps back, you inch closer. Some dads might think, *Fine, if you don't want to hang out with me, I'll find something I'd rather be doing.* But like all women, your daughter wants to be pursued.

Even wooed. (Funny-looking word, isn't it? But very powerful!) So keep entering her space and asking her on mini-dates. When she says, "Sure, Dad," go ahead and make a little bit of a big deal about it. But not too big.

Soon enough, your relationship will come full circle and your daughter will regularly want your full attention, wisdom, and levelheaded advice regarding many of the weighty and trivial issues facing teenage girls today. Don't miss that moment. Make sure you're available because—as always—she'll be counting on her dad.

Takeaway

The greatest father–daughter dance is not when the kindergartner balances on your shoes or when the bride puts her head on your shoulder. The greatest father–daughter dance happens between those two milestones as you gracefully enter her world with wisdom and love, depart with diplomacy, and enter again and again with perfect harmony and timing.

"When I was a child, I spoke and thought and reasoned as a child. But when I grew up, I put away childish things."

—1 CORINTHIANS 13:11 NLT

A Daughter Needs Her Dad…

To Let Her Know She Makes You Proud

For 32 years, my dad was principal at Harrison Street School, the only elementary school on the east side of Geneva, Illinois. Growing up, his four children—Mary Kay, Mark, Jay, and Sue—often heard some version of this statement, "Oh, you must be related to Ken Payleitner, the principal. Is he your dad?" And that was fine. He was admired and respected by his staff and students. The question was never embarrassing, but as a goofy nine-year-old I never knew how to respond.

My older sister, Mary Kay, spent more time in and around Geneva and heard that question more than any of us. After graduating college, Mary Kay began a successful real-estate career serving the Geneva area and was never surprised when someone asked if she was related to Ken Payleitner.

One summer a young family moved to town. They appreciated my sister's above-and-beyond efforts to find them just the right house on the east side of Geneva. As fall approached, that mom went to register her kindergartner at the local elementary school and happened to meet the principal. Of course she said, "Oh, you must be related to Mary Kay Payleitner, the real-estate agent." My dad didn't miss a beat. He puffed up his chest a little and said, "Why, yes—that's my daughter. She's one of the best real-estate agents in town."

The story doesn't end there. After new-student registration was over that day, the principal sat down and wrote a short note to the real-estate agent. It began, "Dearest daughter, you made me proud today…" And in his note he shared the above scenario.

The story still doesn't end there. Back in the mid-1970s, the salaries of school administrators in the Chicago suburbs were modest. As a matter of fact, a hardworking young realtor could actually earn a higher annual income than an elementary-school principal. In her second or third year in the real estate business, that's what happened to my sister. I'm not sure how those financial figures were revealed, but when they came out my dad sat down and wrote another note to his oldest daughter. It began, "Dearest Mary Kay, You make me proud..."

Dad, I know you want your daughter to do well. To succeed. To do great things. But would it be okay with you if she made more money than you? Would that bruise your male ego? Even if your little girl is still a little girl, you need to look at her and think, *Yes, that would be okay...that would be fantastic...I would be proud.*

Backing up, the most relevant point to this story of my dad and my sister from more than three decades ago might be this: Keep paper, envelopes, stamps, and an up-to-date address book handy. We may not be able to save the U.S. Postal Service, but we can certainly take advantage of the remarkable opportunity we have to put an envelope in the little box in front of our house and have it end up a few days later in the hands of our daughter who is off at camp, in a college dorm, at a military base, in an apartment, or wherever life has taken her. If she's still living in a bedroom down the hallway, you might even consider leaving a handwritten note in an envelope on her pillow.

If you're not sure what to write, consider starting with these proven words: "Dearest daughter, you make me proud..."

Takeaway

My father perfected his elegant yet masculine handwriting under the watchful eye of the nuns back in parochial school in the 1930s. After he passed away last year, we found a box of love letters he had written to my mom in 1948 and 1949. All in the same disciplined, flowing script. Men, even though you do all your writing at a keyboard now, I urge you to grab a real pen once in a while and write a note to your daughter in real ink to mark a special occasion, share some encouragement, or just to say "I love you."

"I thank my God every time I remember you."
—Philippians 1:3

A Daughter Needs Her Dad…

To Expect Food Battles

This will happen. Your daughter will stare at a wonderful plate filled with beef, potatoes, and vegetables and seemingly out-of-the-blue declare, "I can't eat this. I'm on a diet."

Dad, I know you would never say, "Well, fatty, it's about time you lost a few pounds." But you need to know that many of the things you would say will be interpreted exactly that way.

Consider these responses: "That's great, sweetie." "Carly, you look fine the way you are." "Most boys like a girl with curves." "Well, what *can* you eat?" "Your mother made this meal—you're going to eat it." "You are not going on a diet. No one expects you to look like a supermodel." Dad, each of these statements could be taken totally the wrong way. You've never been a 14-year-old girl. You need to know there's a difference between what you intend to say and what your daughter hears.

So how do you respond when your daughter declares, "I'm going on a diet"? Like most interactions with your growing daughter, you want to hear what she's really thinking. And that might require you to do something you may not be very good at: listening. The good news is that if you let your daughter know that you really do want to hear what she has to say, there's a good chance she'll start talking. Boys won't do that. Girls will.

So maybe the best response is something like, "Well, I guess we could all eat a little healthier. What kind of diet are you thinking about?" The goal is to get the topic out in the open and then, Dad, shut up and listen.

But be warned. If she's already on the slippery slope of an eating disorder, she may not want to talk about it. The cover-up and denial have already begun. As difficult as it may sound, the hunger pangs and desperate need to lose more and more weight are a part of her life in which she finds comfort and meaning. You—the dad who loves her more than life itself—are an outsider who doesn't understand. When she gets angry with you, it's the disease talking.

But these statistics might make it clearer:[4]

- An estimated 10 million American women suffer from eating disorders.
- 81 percent of 10-year-olds are afraid of being fat.
- 25 percent of college-age women engage in bingeing and purging as a weight-management technique.
- 20 percent of people suffering from anorexia will die prematurely from complications related to their eating disorder, including suicide and heart problems.

Again, it's worth reminding all dads that girls of every shape and size are going to have these emotions and struggles. If your daughter is crazy skinny, don't think she's immune. As a matter of fact, girls who are size 0 or size 2 are prime candidates for anorexia or bulimia.

You should also be aware of a disturbing and growing pro-anorexia subculture. Blogs and websites using terms like *thinspiration* and *pro-ana* are filled with advice for girls about diet pills, raising your metabolism, training yourself to hate food, and identifying foods that generate "negative calories." The sites are not secretive. These bloggers are proud of promoting the goal of becoming a living skeleton.

If you think there's even a chance that your daughter is bingeing, purging, exercising too much, or not getting the nutrition she needs, you need to take action. Too much is at stake. This short chapter cannot begin to give you the information or action points you need. Dad, do what you have to do. Do the research. Talk to doctors. Be the heroic father your little girl needs.

Finally, even if your daughter is healthy and eating well, this chapter should serve as a reminder of how severe this problem is with an alarming number of young ladies. Tragically so.

Takeaway

When your daughter begins her food battles, don't join in. Remain neutral, Dad. Come alongside and love her. She's already under enough pressure from peers, boys, social expectations, and her own imagination.

> *"Every weight-loss program, no matter how positively it's packaged, whispers to you that you're not right. You're not good enough. You're unacceptable and you need to be fixed."*
>
> —KIM BRITTINGHAM

A Daughter Needs Her Dad…

To Referee Between the Two Most Important Women in Your Life

Quick, who are the two most important women in your life?

Got an answer? If you said your mom and grandmother, you are way off. If you said your mom and your wife, that's a little closer. But for any dad reading this book, the answer must be "My bride and my daughter."

If you have not yet cut the apron strings, you need to close this book right now, call Mommy and tell her that you love her dearly, but from now on she is in third place in your heart. (Or fourth, fifth, or sixth if you have more than one daughter.)

Now back to your sweet wife and your even-more-sweet daughter. The two of them are going to have a relationship quite different from any you have ever witnessed. In the early years, the mother–daughter relationship boasts a wonderful innocence. "When I grow up, I want to be just like you, Mommy!" But as soon as a growing girl looks in the mirror and begins to see her mother, that all changes.

During the second decade of a girl's life she and her mother are best friends and worst enemies. And you're caught in the middle, Dad. Sometimes those two women will be adversarial. Sometimes conspiratorial. Often, you will be required to choose sides. Just as often, you may have to defend yourself from their double-barreled verbal assaults on your character, manhood, or ability to trust, provide, protect, and love. Long ago, your daughter and her mom each developed her own method for getting you to do what she wants you to do. Even if you didn't realize it.

Daughters tend to coo, smile demurely, and appeal to your generous spirit and male ego. Sometimes female offspring rely on the age-old ploy of flying into a tantrum or pouting until they get their way. Wives use all those weapons but also have years of history to throw in your face—plus, of course, the ability to withhold romantic favors.

On what subjects might you need to take sides? Curfews. Boys. Friends you don't like. Friends you don't know. Wardrobe. A slightly messy room. A room with a floor you can't see because it's covered with unidentifiable items of clothing. Freedom vs. limits. Ultimatums vs. requests. Dreams vs. reality.

The best course of action is almost always the united front. When it comes to matters of consequence, parents need to stick together and provide a reasonable and justifiable case for why their collective decades of experience and wisdom trump teenage immaturity. (Caution: Never use the word *immature* with any child. You're asking for six months of noncommunication.)

You can and should disagree with and debate your daughter's mom behind closed doors. Remind your wife about teenage boys. Let her remind you about teenage girls. Share insights, fears, gut feelings, and warning signs. Go on fact-finding missions that glean knowledge from other parents, online parenting forums, biblically based resources, and youth pastors. Certainly, allow your daughter to present her case. Together or separately listen to her point of view. When she says, "Dad, Mom won't listen to me. Can you talk to her?" you can promise that you will do exactly that. But when the time comes, make sure you and Mom are on the same page. As co-parents, you need to decide and firmly present what the two of you truly believe is the best for your daughter. In the short and long term.

Will your parenting ultimatums change over time? Absolutely. As your daughter demonstrates maturity, she should be granted more freedom and more responsibility. When the actions of your child demonstrate they understand the idea of delayed gratification, you can better trust them to make decisions that will serve them over time.

Still, it's good to know there are two of you watching out for your daughter's well-being. You're a unified parenting team. Then, when your little girl makes a not-so-good decision, neither of you can look at the other and say, "I told you so."

Takeaway

Daughters will play you, Dad. They will say things like "Don't you trust me?" or "Please, Daddy, just this one time." When that happens, remember the temptations and challenges of your own teenage years. And know that each generation faces everything that threatened the previous generation. Plus another entire layer of risks and hazards.

> *"What causes fights and quarrels among you? Don't they come from your desires that battle within you? You desire but do not have, so you kill. You covet but you cannot get what you want, so you quarrel and fight. You do not have because you do not ask God."*
>
> —JAMES 4:1-2

A Daughter Needs Her Dad...

To Recall Fondly the Unfortunate Incident at the FBI Building

One dad, one mom, five kids. One minivan. Driving from Chicago to Washington, DC, to experience our nation's capital. Our oldest, Alec, is heading into his senior year of high school. Rae Anne is four. The three middle children—Randy, Max, and Isaac—engage in constantly changing levels of mutual love, laughter, and pounding.

The budget and schedule are both tight. At the crack of dawn, I leave our hotel room and drive to the Federal Triangle. The plan is for me to acquire time-stamped tickets to the White House for later that morning and swing back and pick up my relaxed and well-rested family. The timing is perfect, except for one small hitch. The White House is closed for public tours that day.

I overcome my frustration by jogging three blocks and securing the coveted position of third in line for the tour of the FBI building, which features lots of guns and secret agent stuff. Not a bad second choice. The doors are scheduled to open in 45 minutes, which I figure is plenty of time for Rita to get the crew up, dressed, and through the very-easy-to-navigate Metro. As scores of tourists begin to line up behind me, I call Rita with very specific instructions about where, when, and how to get to my location outside the FBI gates. Piece of cake, right?

I wasn't there, but Rita tells a slightly different story. Alec heroically gets his brothers ready to go. My wife wrestles our young and feisty daughter into a cute little outfit. Hand in hand, the six of them hustle over to, down in, on, off, and up from the Metro. A couple blocks from the FBI building, sweet Rae Anne stops in her tracks, yanks her hands out from the grasp of her mom and oldest brother, and fiercely asks the timely and astute question, "What's a vacation again?"

At the time it wasn't funny. But as you may imagine, the story has taken on a life of its own. Even now, when a family member schedules too many activities during a long weekend they'll stop in their tracks and do their best impression of four-year-old Rae Anne: "What's a vacation again?"

The story actually doesn't end there. At about the time my family is zooming through subterranean DC, the tour guides at the FBI building decide to open the gates early, and literally hundreds of tourists funnel past me, queuing up for their turn inside. My cherished third place in line is a moot point by the time my family reaches my side. Our tour finally begins some two hours later. Like I said, it wasn't funny at the time. I guess you had to be there.

But hopefully you *have* been there. Hopefully, you have been part of emotionally charged events that resulted in classic family stories told again and again. You see, there's no way Rae Anne can remember that so-called vacation or the first time she uttered that now-famous family catchphrase. She was only four. But she has heard the tale so many times, it has become part of her mental file cabinet of family memories.

Allow me to take this idea one step farther. Today, Rae Anne is confident in her ability to speak truth into a difficult or challenging situation. She knows her words carry weight and wisdom. Indeed, when she has something to say, people listen. Peers, teammates, coaches, officers, professors. Without overstating the case, it just might be that hearing her parents tell the story of a little girl with a wisdom beyond her years has given Rae Anne the poise and sense of conviction that serves her so well today.

I am taking no credit. All I did was drive a jam-packed minivan to DC and learn to laugh about it in the years afterward.

Takeaway

So much of life is a matter of perspective. I wouldn't trade the memory of those three days in our nation's capital for anything. If you had asked me in the middle of it, I might have had a different answer.

> *"'Do you hear what these children are saying?' they asked him.
> 'Yes,' replied Jesus, 'have you never read, "From the lips of children
> and infants you, Lord, have called forth your praise"?'"*
>
> —MATTHEW 21:16

A Daughter Needs Her Dad...

To Introduce Her to the Proverbs 31 Woman

Some claim the Bible is repressive toward females, misogynistic, anti-woman. Well, anyone who says that simply hasn't read it.

Female heroes of the Bible abound, including Rahab, Miriam, Deborah, Jael, Esther, Ruth, Dorcas, Anna, Mary, Elizabeth, Mary Magdalene, and many others. The Bible describes scores of strong and faithful wives and mothers. But many acts of heroism extended beyond family relationships. One woman hid spies, another drove a tent stake into the head of the commander of the Canaanite army, others were prophets and civic leaders, and one even said, "May it be to me as you have said" when an angel told her she would give birth to the Son of God.

Beyond those specific role models, you can find more biblical proof that women have potential for extraordinary purpose and value. The last page of Proverbs explains how a woman is instrumental to the economic, spiritual, and physical welfare of her family and her community. Read it for yourself.

> A wife of noble character who can find?
>   She is worth far more than rubies.
> Her husband has full confidence in her
>   and lacks nothing of value.
> She brings him good, not harm,
>   all the days of her life.
> She selects wool and flax

and works with eager hands.
She is like the merchant ships,
    bringing her food from afar.
She gets up while it is still night;
    she provides food for her family
    and portions for her female servants.
She considers a field and buys it;
    out of her earnings she plants a vineyard.
She sets about her work vigorously;
    her arms are strong for her tasks.
She sees that her trading is profitable,
    and her lamp does not go out at night.
In her hand she holds the distaff
    and grasps the spindle with her fingers.
She opens her arms to the poor
    and extends her hands to the needy.
When it snows, she has no fear for her household;
    for all of them are clothed in scarlet.
She makes coverings for her bed;
    she is clothed in fine linen and purple.
Her husband is respected at the city gate,
    where he takes his seat among the elders of the land.
She makes linen garments and sells them,
    and supplies the merchants with sashes.
She is clothed with strength and dignity;
    she can laugh at the days to come.
She speaks with wisdom,
    and faithful instruction is on her tongue.
She watches over the affairs of her household
    and does not eat the bread of idleness.
Her children arise and call her blessed;
    her husband also, and he praises her:
"Many women do noble things,
    but you surpass them all."
Charm is deceptive, and beauty is fleeting;
    but a woman who fears the LORD is to be praised.

Honor her for all that her hands have done,
and let her works bring her praise at the city gate.

That is one impressive woman. Maybe, Dad, set this book aside and spend the next few months doing a line-by-line Scripture study with your daughter about the wife of noble character described here. The Bible spells out some high expectations. Underline these specific phrases in your own study Bible. Noble character. Lacks nothing of value. Eager hands. Work vigorously. Strength and dignity. Speaks with wisdom. Fears the Lord.

Notice that those character traits aren't passive. They're proactive. Her actions lead to great rewards for her family. A confident husband. Provisions for her family from around the world. Real-estate holdings. Healthy crops. Wise investments. Outreach to the poor. Warm clothes in winter. Entrepreneurial garment-making. A sense of humor. Kids who respect her. A husband who praises her in public.

Like your daughter, the Proverbs 31 woman is nothing short of spectacular. As a matter of fact, much of the chit chat down at the city center is about this gal's awesomeness. Some are even saying that since she's so fantastic, her husband must also have his act together.

Such is the power of a noble woman. It's all right there in your daughter's study Bible. If she doesn't have one, order one today and present it to her with an encouraging word and a bookmark at Proverbs 31.

Takeaway

Say this to your daughter, "Put God first, and you can be anything you want to be." Few girls hear that from their dad.

"Everyone has inside of her a piece of good news. The good news is that you don't know how great you can be! How much you can love! What you can accomplish! And what your potential is!"

—ANNE FRANK

A Daughter Needs Her Dad…

To Fill Her Room with Balloons

Kicking around this book, I talked to lots of dads and lots of daughters. Sometimes as individuals, sometimes together. The questions that always got the biggest responses were fairly straightforward: "Tell me about your dad" or "Tell me about your daughter."

My survey was random and unofficial. I rarely took word-for-word notes. But in their responses, recurring themes left me with bittersweet emotions. As I spoke with daughters who had moved out years ago and were now grown women, there was typically a long pause, a slight head tilt, and a faraway look as they seemed to search through a storehouse of memories. When finally speaking, they would almost always begin with a positive statement but finish with the intimation of unfinished business.

"He worked hard. And often told me how pretty I was. I only see him a couple times a year now."

"He had a great sense of humor and loved being with our family until it just became too hard for him."

"My dad supported me in everything I did. But it never seemed like I was doing what he wanted me to do. Maybe it was all in my imagination."

Older dads tended to brag on their daughters, never took credit, and usually expressed some kind of regret.

"Sara had so much talent in so many areas. By the time she was in high school, I couldn't keep up with her."

"My daughter and my wife were very much alike. Sometimes I felt like I was on the outside looking in. But seeing them together made me happy."

"She's an intern at a hospital in Dallas. She's got ten times the brains and compassion that I ever had."

Some of my most fascinating informal research occurred at airports, especially during flight delays. Most amusing were growing families with dads and daughters sitting together. Questions were almost always answered with a wisecrack and a giggle. The response to "Tell me about your daughter" was an easy setup for a fatherly punch line:

"When she's not playing Angry Birds, she's actually a fairly charming human being."

"She's smart. She's beautiful. She's got lots of friends. And her bedroom is immaculate. Well, three out of four isn't so bad."

My favorite responses may have been when daughters were talking about their dads who were sitting right beside them. The dads were often surprised. Girls seemed eager to compliment their dads...with a twist.

"Well, he tells jokes that are not funny and he comes to all my games and recitals and I think I do better when he's around."

"My daddy reads to me and I read to him. When we talk he looks at me and really listens, and I like that."

"My dad helps me most when he's not around. I'll be making a tough decision and I'll hear his voice in my head and that's how I decide what to do."

Not long ago, at Denver International, I struck up a conversation with a family headed home to Salt Lake City from Orlando. After only a brief moment of thought, the ten-year-old daughter gave this response to my generic question: "He makes a big deal about my birthday." The dad looked quizzical and so I asked for an example. She said, "One year he filled my bedroom with balloons." A few follow-up questions revealed the whole story. The birthday-balloon surprise had been three years earlier. The balloons were actually mom's idea. And mom blew up most of them.

Interesting, don't you think?

Their flight number was called, I autographed one of my books for the dad, and that family of four was on their way leaving me to ponder the words of that young girl. "He makes a big deal about my birthday."

Of all the things she could have said, that's what she wanted her dad to hear. That was a memory she cherished. It was orchestrated and executed by mom. But the daughter was giving credit to the dad.

Did you hear the subtext? Did you hear what that girl was really saying and really hoping for? I did. I hope that dad did. I'm pretty sure she was saying, "Thanks, Daddy, for making me feel special. Please do it again."

Takeaway

Partner with your daughter's mom. Orchestrate memories. Don't settle for a sparse bunch of five or six balloons. Sometimes go a little overboard. Finally, imagine what your daughter might say if a strange author in a crowded airport asked, "Tell me about your dad."

> *"A child's eyes, those clear wells of undefiled thought—what on earth can be more beautiful? Full of hope, love and curiosity, they meet your own. In prayer, how earnest; in joy, how sparkling; in sympathy, how tender! The man who never tried the companionship of a little child has carelessly passed by one of the great pleasures of life, as one passes a rare flower without plucking it or knowing its value."*
>
> —CAROLINE NORTON

A Daughter Needs Her Dad...

To Be Scared to Death for Her

D ad, you need to be scared for your daughter. Because there's a good chance she isn't scared at all.

You raised her to be strong, confident, and optimistic and make good decisions. As a result, her character is strong. Her confidence is admirable. She has a positive outlook. Her decision-making ability is exceptional. However, there's one thing she doesn't have. Experience.

It's not your fault, Dad. Experience comes from...well, experience. Not just your own—over the years you've also taken in quite a bit of secondhand knowledge from the many candid and honest adult conversations you've had with friends, co-workers, guys in your small group, and family members. It turns out that bad things sometimes happen to teenage girls. If God has spared your daughter from traumatic experiences, you certainly know other families who have not been so fortunate. In addition, a little online research, reading the local paper, and watching the evening news will confirm that we need to be afraid. To be very afraid.

We live in a fallen world. Every one of us is one or two degrees of separation away from every father's nightmare(s). Runaway kids. Head-on collisions. Teenage pregnancies. Sexually transmitted diseases. Anorexia. Bulimia. Suicide. Offspring who are addicts, shoplifters, or institutionalized. We all know good families in which teenagers have lost their innocence or their lives. The only logical response for caring fathers like you and me is fear.

Before we get offtrack, let's pause for a moment and consider a few definitions of the word *fear*.

1. Awe and respect for God is one kind of fear. Psalm 111:10 tells us that "the fear of the LORD is the beginning of wisdom; all who follow his precepts have good understanding." That's a good, healthy fear we want to hang on to.

2. Another kind of fear is a sense of hopelessness as we experience disappointments and loss in this fallen world. At the Last Supper, Jesus promised us a peace that surpasses all understanding. He told his disciples, "Peace I leave with you; my peace I give you. I do not give to you as the world gives. Do not let your hearts be troubled and do not be afraid" (John 14:27). Ultimately, we can cast aside our greatest fears and claim eternal victory because we have an all-powerful God on our side.

3. Then, there's the actuating fear God places in our hearts as a motivator. It's not paralyzing, it's empowering. It's a reminder to be on watch for any dark forces that threaten you and your family. That's when you and I are called to "be on your guard; stand firm in the faith; be courageous; be strong" (1 Corinthians 16:13).

Personally, for my daughter and yours, I cannot stop being afraid. And I'm grateful to God for that feeling. As fathers, our job is to be on guard and be courageous. Being aware of the dangers of the world motivates me to stay close to Rae Anne. To encourage her in pursuing noble ideals and worthy goals. To remind her how valuable, beautiful, and cherished she is. Even sometimes to test her by reminding her of the presence of evil and seeing how she responds.

I recommend that you also allow yourself to be motivated by the scary, scary world. Don't stick your head in the sand. Instead, protect your daughter by providing her with information, perspective, a listening ear, and unconditional love. Your efforts will not be wasted.

Regretfully, for many dads it's a losing battle. They're not prepared to fight for their daughters and falsely believe that they can wish away the demons or, worse, that the demons don't exist. Even dads who do have a battle plan often dangerously underestimate the power of the enemy.

If your daughter knows the Savior, I completely understand how you don't live in fear for her eternal destination. When it comes to my own daughter, I share that confidence. But we've also been given the responsibility to protect our families and provide them with opportunities to fulfill God's call on their lives here on earth. Knowing the dangers your daughter faces and fiercely protecting her through her teenage years and well into her twenties will go a long way toward opening doors to the joy-filled life God has waiting for her.

Takeaway

If fear is paralyzing you and your family, then ignore the dark undertones of this chapter. Don't dwell on your fears and anxieties. Instead, pledge to live more confidently and boldly in the provision and protection promised by the Lord. Claim victory in his name.

*"Our problem is not to be rid of fear but
rather to harness and master it."*

—Martin Luther King Jr.

A Daughter Needs Her Dad…

To Knock and Pray

Here's an idea I stole from another dad. He said it was okay.

Anytime day or night, knock on your daughter's bedroom door and say something like, "I need a quiet place to pray. Can I jump in here for about two minutes?" She may look up and blink a couple times, but I am pretty sure her response will be, "Umm. I guess so."

Then, do it. Walk in, sit on the edge of her bed, and almost as if she's not there start praying right out loud, but in a low tone of voice. Pray for your situation at work, your wife, your other kids, your own stresses, a neighbor, your community, and any other concerns you might have. End with a prayer for your daughter, who is sitting right there with you. Thank her, kiss her forehead, and leave quietly and gracefully.

Is that something you can do? Does that sound impossible? If you can't imagine that scene taking place, allow me to give you an example of what your words might sound like.

"Heavenly Father, thank you for your generosity and the love you keep pouring on our family. I'm humbled and grateful. I'm challenged to serve you as best I can. You know how the media-management project at work is stressing me out, Lord, and I need to ask you for some patience and some new direction. If you could guide my work this week, that would be great. For my family, Lord, you know Tim is waiting to hear back about those college applications. Help him trust you and make the right choice for next fall. And for Tammy, help me be the husband she needs. What a gift she is to me and our kids. Please, God, continue to bless our marriage. For Mr. Bradley's surgery. For safe travels next

week as I head to Pittsburgh. For the election next month. Lord, please let your will be done in all these areas. Finally, for Megan. You've given her such a tender heart for others and a great sense of humor. Thank you, Lord. Help her to turn to you for all her decisions. Protect her always. I pray this in the name of your Son, Jesus. Amen."

Now that wasn't so hard, was it? Your daughter may have been stunned by the experience. Or maybe it made perfect sense to her.

In any case, that two minutes you spent in your daughter's room achieves about a dozen worthy goals. You prayed. You modeled how to pray. You let your daughter know that you believe prayer works. You entered your daughter's world. You allowed her to enter your world. You let her know that your marriage is strong. You reminded her that other members of the family have concerns that are equal to or greater than hers. You let her know your schedule. And maybe your prayers helped unleash some supernatural forces—such as legions of guardian angels—within the walls of her bedroom.

Perhaps best of all, you have earned the right to return in the near future to knock and pray again. My friend related that, at first, his unannounced prayer visits were a bit of an intrusion into his daughter's adolescent world, but he told her it was his responsibility as a father and she'd have to get used to it. Over the months and years, he began to pray for her heart, health, friends, future, and even her future husband, whoever that might be. At first, she just listened. Then she began to add her own prayers. Sometimes the prayer time led to an extended conversation about significant issues—conversations that might otherwise have never taken place.

Through it all, that young woman began to understand and appreciate the act of surrender her dad was demonstrating. This man she looked up to and respected had a greater confidence in his heavenly Father than he had in his own strength and abilities. As he cast all his cares onto God, she realized this was something she could do as well. Her own trust in God grew exponentially.

I'm betting you already do bedtime prayers with your daughter. But you must admit, sometimes they become repetitive and uninspired. I urge you to go ahead and engage in some risky prayer. Pray big. Pray expectantly. And try some unannounced prayer. Just knock and pray.

Takeaway

Your children all need to understand the passage from 2 Corinthians 12:10 that says, "When I am weak, then I am strong." But I think girls especially need to see that their daddy depends on his heavenly Father.

> *"When you pray, go into your room, close the door and pray to your Father, who is unseen. Then your Father, who sees what is done in secret, will reward you. And when you pray, do not keep on babbling like pagans, for they think they will be heard because of their many words. Do not be like them, for your Father knows what you need before you ask him."*
>
> —Jesus, in Matthew 6:6-8

A Daughter Needs Her Dad...

To Surrender to the American Girl Thing

I've lost track of where the stores are. It doesn't matter to me anymore. But for a few years, Rae Anne was into American Girl. I must say it was fun, healthy, age-appropriate, educational, and a little pricey.

Actually it wasn't break-the-bank expensive. It was just more than seemed necessary to spend on one doll or one outfit. And those accessories, books, and gadgets can add up. So, if you open the door to an American Girl store, explore their website, or allow one of their catalogs into your home, keep your credit card fully loaded. Truthfully, like most shopping excursions you take with your daughter, you'll want to treat each purchase as a teachable moment.

Think of it as setting some ground rules for the next decade. If she really wants the gingham jumper and the plaid sweater vest with matching skirt for Molly, respectfully suggest she choose one outfit or the other. If she simply must have the accessory pack, three adventure books, and the DVD, say "No, I don't think so" and then secretly order those items and tuck them away for Christmas or her next birthday. If she throws herself on the floor of the store screaming that she must have the entire wardrobe and absolutely every Molly accessory, leave immediately and without apology.

By the way, Molly is a pretty good choice when you steer your daughter toward one particular American Girl doll. All the characters appear to be about nine-to-eleven years old, and many of them represent different eras in U.S. history, from colonial times through the Depression to even the long-lost disco era. Molly McIntire is described as "a patriotic girl growing up during World War Two." Short films and books chronicle her adventures during 1944, which include volunteering for the Red Cross, tending a victory garden, and receiving a telegram that her father is missing in action. Molly opens the door to all kinds of conversations about patriotism, sacrifice, history, and family.

I'm not shilling for American Girl. They're doing pretty well without my help. I'm just saying that dolls and dads can mix. And you need to be aware of trends and fads, and help your daughter make reasonable and informed decisions. Sometimes you may even have to do a little research—or at the very least, be aware of the cultural and spiritual implications.

Case in point. In 2009, American Girl added a doll named "Gwen Thompson" to their line. Gwen was homeless, living in a car with her mom. The apparent goal was to draw attention to the 1.5 million children living on the street in the U.S. That's an honorable goal, but you can probably see the irony of a family spending a hundred bucks on that particular doll and accessories. American Girl corporate decisions have sparked other controversies over the years, which even led to some boycotts. As with many organizations that cater to girls—including the Girls Scouts of America—there are links to feminist organizations that lead to links to pro-abortion organizations and other groups that may not share your values.

All this makes me very glad that you, Dad, are proactively involved in the life of your daughter. Be there to help answer the easy questions about which doll to buy and which bedtime book to read. That way you'll have lots of practice as the questions get more challenging and the answers more critical.

Takeaway

Your daughter may go through fads and stages like wildfire. Dolls. Barbie dolls. Boots. Gymnastics. Soccer. Poetry. Pez dispensers. Ponies. Purses. Vampires. Boy bands. Toe rings. Sock monkeys. Scarves. Skateboards. Tattoos. As frightening as that sounds, you'll want to be aware of every stage and give it your blessing. Or help bring it to a reasonable conclusion.

"Little girls love dolls. They just don't love doll clothes. We've got four thousand dolls and ain't one of them got a stitch of clothes on."

—Jeff Foxworthy

A Daughter Needs Her Dad...

To Walk Her Down the Aisle

Don't bring any regrets to your daughter's day.

All the emotions, money concerns, decisions, nervousness, and eagerness surrounding your daughter's wedding day already bring enough drama. As father of the bride, you need to do everything possible to dulcify the day and all the planning leading up to it. You need to be both a rock and a rock star. When everyone around you is scurrying and worrying about details, you need to see the big picture of what's really going on. The day is not about you, but you have the power to make or break it. You've certainly seen *Father of the Bride* (1991) with Steve Martin or *Father of the Bride* (1950) with Spencer Tracy. If not, put this book down, find a DVD or download one of those movies, and watch it with your daughter in the next 72 hours.

Hollywood scriptwriters got it right. When your little girl announces her engagement, your relationship changes forever. She's about to give her heart to some guy who is barely worthy to be in the same room with her, and all you can do is offer congratulations and keep saying some version of "Anything you want, sweetheart. Anything you want."

With that essential business taken care of, let's switch gears. Wedding planning, wedding jitters, who's on the guest list, and who's pulling out their credit cards are not the topic of this chapter. The topic—like every chapter in this book—is you and your daughter.

Dad, have you earned the right to walk her down the aisle? For most of the men reading this book, that's a no-brainer. "She's my daughter. My angel. My joy. We're very close. For 20-some years, I've been pouring my heart into hers. Escorting her down the aisle of that church or garden path will be one of the most wondrous and most difficult things I will ever do."

But that's not the case for all dads. Statistics tell a different story. Quite a few of you are stepfathers trying to figure out how you fit into the life of a girl who still has a birth father living across town or three states away. Some of you are working hard to regain the respect of your daughter, which was lost because of regrettable decisions you've made over the years. Some of you are replacing a man who died young. Some of you are not legal fathers or custodial fathers at all, but you know a girl who needs an adult-male role model in her life and you're stepping up to the task. I applaud all of you. I salute any man who has dedicated a portion of his life to modeling how a Christian man treats a woman. With respect, honor, gentleness, and love.

For every father or father figure reading these words, my prayer is that you find authentic joy in your relationship with your daughter or "daughter." As my favorite psalm affirms, "Children are a gift from the LORD; they are a reward from him" (Psalm 127:3 NLT). Your job is to accept that gift and then give her right back to God. And sometimes that includes giving her away in marriage.

Finally, the real purpose of this chapter. If for any reason that bride you care about so much does not invite you to walk her down the aisle on her wedding day, you need to convey zero amount of guilt her direction. I repeat...zero. Your daughter, stepdaughter, niece, granddaughter, sister, or special friend may have already agonized over a very tough decision, and you need to be ready with a heroic response. If it comes up, take her aside, look at her beautiful face, and tell her you love her and that it's not a problem at all. If it never comes up, don't bring it up. Just keep smiling and celebrate the day.

Of course, no man—even the best dad in the world—should ever take that privilege for granted. Sometime before, during, or after the wedding celebration, thank your daughter for the honor. In return, the least you can do is promise to pray for her and her new husband every day for the rest of your life. And then do it.

My number-three son, Max, got married just last summer. His bride,

Megan, gave me permission to include this note she wrote to her father the week before their wedding.

> *Dad,*
>
> *You were the first man I loved, and although a lot of things are changing now, that never will. Thank you for leading me through this beautiful life and preparing me for this day.*
>
> > *Love,*
> > *Your Little Girl*

Congratulations, Dave. You got it right. And you've given thousands of other dads something to shoot for.

Takeaway

Remember: step, together, step, together, step, together. Or whatever they tell you to do.

> *"You fathers will understand. You have a little girl. An adorable little girl who looks up to you and adores you in a way you could never have imagined. I remember how her little hand used to fit inside mine. Then comes the day when she wants to get her ears pierced, and wants you to drop her off a block before the movie theater. From that moment on you're in a constant panic. You worry about her meeting the wrong kind of guy, the kind of guy who only wants one thing, and you know exactly what that one thing is, because it's the same thing you wanted when you were their age. Then, you stop worrying about her meeting the wrong guy, and you worry about her meeting the right guy. That's the greatest fear of all, because, then you lose her."*

—Steve Martin as George Banks in *Father of the Bride* (1991); screenplay by Frances Goodrich, Albert Hackett, Nancy Meyers, and Charles Shyer

A Daughter Needs Her Dad…

To Place Her Hand in the Groom's Hand

It's a moving scene. A dad escorts a blushing bride down through gathered family and friends to the front of the church, where the preacher makes a few comments and then says something like, "Who gives this woman to be wedded to this man?"

Those words have a nice traditional ambience, but like most modern dads I hesitate to take ownership of another human being, even if she is my own flesh and blood. What's more, the idea that I am giving her away seems a bit out-of-date. But is it?

Let's see what Scripture says.

Proverbs 19:14 reminds the mother and father of the bride, "Houses and wealth are inherited from parents, but a prudent wife is from the LORD." That would indicate that the girl walking down the aisle in the white gown belongs first and foremost to God. You've helped shape her, Dad, but she's not really "yours" to give away.

As we meet Adam and Eve, Genesis 2:24 tells us, "A man leaves his father and mother and is united to his wife, and they become one flesh." That revealing verse seems to be primarily a reminder to the groom to make his new family a priority over his old family, especially cutting the apron strings from Mom. It's the powerful confirmation that brides and especially grooms need to leave and cleave.

So where does the idea of "giving away the bride" come from? It most likely goes back to the days of arranged marriages and dowries, by virtue of which a woman's family would actually transfer some amount of money or estate to the groom or his family. I understand dowries are still part of the package in some parts of the world, but that sounds more like a financial transaction than a healthy way to start a marriage.

In Christian circles, the idea of "giving away the bride" may extend to that hornet's nest known as *submission*. Ephesians 5:22 says, "Wives, submit yourselves to your own husbands as you do to the Lord." A traditional but not biblical understanding of that idea is that a girl has been under the complete control of her father and that control is about to be transferred to her new husband.

Let's take a fresh look at that verse and see what a dad should be doing to get his daughter ready to approach her marriage from a biblical perspective. As always, it's a good idea to read biblical passages in context. Ephesians 5:21—the nine words immediately preceding that verse—says quite plainly, "Submit to one another out of reverence for Christ." That's pretty clear. The apostle Paul was writing to believers in the church at Ephesus and all believers everywhere. Husbands, wives, fathers, mothers, sons, and daughters should all seek to have the heart of a servant and put first the needs of others.

In the next dozen or so verses, Paul explains the formula for building a family. A husband needs to live for and be ready to die for his bride. A wife needs to feel cherished and marry a man whom she will trust to lead. Kids need wise instruction. Read it for yourself:

> Husbands, love your wives, just as Christ loved the church and gave himself up for her (Ephesians 5:25).

> Wives, submit yourselves to your own husbands as you do to the Lord. For the husband is the head of the wife as Christ is the head of the church, his body, of which he is the Savior (Ephesians 5:22-23).

> Children, obey your parents in the Lord, for this is right (Ephesians 6:1).

Dad, you need to do everything you can to make sure your little girl marries a man who is worthy of that trust. Someone who will lead his family with love and wisdom. Someone who will make her feel cherished. Someone who will be a devoted father. Because that's the only formula for marriage that really works.

What if your daughter brings home some schmuck who is not described above? That's a tough one. Hopefully, you will have earned the right to sit down with her—respectfully and with no shouting—and see where that relationship is really going. Ask some open-ended questions about hopes and dreams. Help her picture her life ten years down the road. Help her see her own personal value in your eyes and in the eyes of God.

But the best way to ensure she shows off an engagement ring from some guy who will truly cherish, lead, protect, and provide is to be that kind of guy yourself. Be the kind of husband you want your daughter to have. Be the kind of dad you want your future son-in-law to be. And don't be afraid to set a standard that's tough to match.

So once again, Dad, the pressure's on you. But every effort you make will be worth it on her wedding day and beyond. At the end of that aisle, don't forget to look at your daughter's beautiful face for more than a moment. By that time, nothing more needs to be said. One last kiss on the cheek would be a nice touch. Then turn to that lucky scoundrel that's stealing your little girl's heart and—if you want—look into his face, shake his hand, and say, "Son, you cherish her."

Takeaway

Expect that sometime, somehow your teenage daughter will drive you to the brink of madness. Before you say or do anything you might regret, stop and imagine the moment down the road in which you "give her away." Take a breath. Smile. And then tell her how much you love her. She won't know how to respond.

> *"Love is patient, love is kind. It does not envy, it does not boast, it*
> *is not proud. It does not dishonor others, it is not self-seeking, it*
> *is not easily angered, it keeps no record of wrongs. Love does*
> *not delight in evil but rejoices with the truth. It always protects,*
> *always trusts, always hopes, always perseveres. Love never fails."*
>
> —1 Corinthians 13:4-8

A Daughter Needs Her Dad...

To Get a Little Angry and Protective

This is a chapter I don't want to write. And you don't want to read. So tell you what. I'll keep it short, giving you just a few facts that will hit you right between the eyes. All you have to do is promise me that you won't stick your head in the sand when it comes to sexually transmitted diseases.[5]

- Human papillomavirus (HPV) is unbelievably common among young people. About 25 percent of teenage girls and about 45 percent of women ages 20 to 24 have a genital HPV infection. On many college campuses more than half the women are infected. Many don't even know it.

- Even girls who are "technical virgins" can get HPV. Skin-to-skin contact, heavy petting, and possibly even hand-to-genital contact can spread the infection that can lead to genital warts and various cancers.

- An estimated 1.5 million new cases of chlamydia infection occur every year among 15-to-24-year-olds. Not treated quickly enough, chlamydia spreads through the reproductive tract, causing scarring and damage around the fallopian tubes, which can lead to infertility and ectopic pregnancies.

- HIV/AIDS is still not curable, and 56,000 cases are diagnosed in the U.S. every year. Heterosexual contact leads to more than 30 percent of the new cases.

- More than one million unmarried women between 20 and 24 become pregnant each year. More than 500,000 become single moms. More than 400,000 abort their babies.

Beyond physical reasons, there are emotional, spiritual, and practical reasons for a girl to delay sex. Today, most intelligent and informed girls get brief glimpses of some of the tragic consequences of premarital sex—through friends, the media, and hit-or-miss sex-ed classes. Still, few of them see the bigger picture and the very real benefits of waiting.

When a girl has parents who are proactively encouraging abstinence she has a strong chance of making it through puberty, high school, college, and to her wedding night without becoming infected. At various times, mom and dad should state their case from a few different angles. Talk graphically about infections, genital warts, and cervical cancer. Explain how STDs can lead to scarring that will leave a woman unable to bear children. Explain how failure rates for condoms are as high as 17 percent.[6] Talk about how God designed sex to cement the bond between a wife and her husband. Every sexual encounter outside of marriage weakens that future bonding.

Pray for and with your daughter that God will give her strong convictions and provide her with friends and even boyfriends who share those same convictions. While you're at it, pray for those friends and pray for your daughter's future husband—acknowledging that she may not have met him yet.

Talk about God's design for sex. Open the Scripture and dialogue about how God emphasizes the importance of sexual purity. Wrong choices don't just bring unwanted pregnancy, infections, emotional baggage, and future sterility. Even worse, wrong choices can keep you from the life he has planned for you.

> It is God's will that you should be sanctified: that you should avoid sexual immorality; that each of you should learn to control your own body in a way that is holy and honorable, not in passionate lust like the pagans, who do not know God; and that in this matter no one should wrong or take advantage of a brother or sister. The Lord will punish all those who

commit such sins, as we told you and warned you before. For God did not call us to be impure, but to live a holy life (1 Thessalonians 4:3-7).

Had enough? The medical facts above were all pulled from an excellent resource titled *Girls Uncovered* from Northfield Publishing, which is loaded with even more stomach-knotting research. The spiritual truth is pulled from the Bible, which is loaded with an unlimited amount of insight on relationships and how to lead a life worth living.

Last thought. If your daughter has already lost her virginity, don't you go off the deep end. Open the door for a fresh start. Especially if she comes to you brokenhearted, help her commit to a "secondary virginity." That's another one of the times in which a wise and committed God-fearing father can take something bad and turn it around for good.

Takeaway

Your daughter has very likely heard much of the terror-filled information above. *But she doesn't think it can happen to her.* Guys, it can. And statistically, it will. So ask yourself, what can you do today to protect her heart, soul, mind, and body? Oddly, that uncomfortable conversation will actually bring the two of you closer together.

> *"Many a man wishes he were strong enough to tear a telephone book in half—especially if he has a teenage daughter."*
> —Guy Lombardo

A Daughter Needs Her Dad...

To (Maybe) Ransack Her Room

Let's say your teenage daughter has closed down communications. And you're not sure why.

Maybe it's just your imagination. Maybe the entire family is crazy busy. You, your wife, and all the kids are just so involved in your own stuff that effective communication has merely taken a brief time-out. Maybe her core values are rock solid and this is simply one of those short seasons of life in which all the love you've poured into your daughter will have to sustain her for a while. You're too busy to give any more right now and she's too busy to receive any love anyway.

So maybe everything is fine. Or maybe it isn't fine.

Maybe she has taken several steps toward some dangerous cliff or slippery slope and your only clue is an uneasiness, a foreboding, a feeling that something is just not right. What do you do with that feeling?

First, don't ignore it.

This is one of those times you'll be glad you have a wife with whom you can communicate. Someone who may be your opposite, but who wants what you want. Someone who loves your daughter as much as you do. Someone who will either confirm your suspicions or explain what your teenage daughter is going through because she went through the same thing herself two or three decades ago. If your daughter's mother is not around, you're going to have to work, not twice, but three times as hard to stay on top of the situation.

As Mom and Dad, you need to join forces and begin your investigation.

Talk to other parents. Look for clues. Notice changes in behavior. Keep a private journal of things that don't seem right. Does your daughter have some new friends that make you uncomfortable? Is there money missing from your wallet? Do cell phones go unanswered? Did she unfriend a longtime best friend? Have you caught her in a lie told right to your face? When you look in her eyes, is your little girl still there? When you compare notes with your daughter's mother, what patterns do you discover?

If your concern continues to grow, widen your search by including other people who love your daughter. Identify other caring adults in her life, such as teachers, coaches, neighbors, youth pastors, and the parents of her longtime friends. Maybe include your daughter's siblings. This may feel like you're ganging up on her, but it's just the opposite. You're gathering a team to support, pray for, and perhaps be part of an intervention for your daughter. The goal is to not make false accusations. The goal is to gather facts.

When you know for sure your daughter is out of the house for a while, go ahead and walk into her bedroom and do a 360-degree turn. Take a fresh look at the world she has created, allowing for quirky style and teenage eccentricities. What's on her desk and nightstand? What has she been writing about recently? It may not yet be time to search every corner of her room, but if you do suspect she's into something that may endanger her well-being you have the right and responsibility to get the truth. But remember you've spent a lifetime building her trust, and you shouldn't take that lightly. Don't blow it by getting caught ransacking her room without cause.

On the other hand, if her life is in danger, she *trusts* you to intervene. She *trusts* you to make the hurt stop. Maybe you *should* pull out drawers, overturn mattresses, reach behind books, open every shoebox on every shelf, and go through pockets of jeans thrown on the floor.

Loud and confrontational accusations based on unsubstantiated suspicions are rarely helpful. She will close you out and leave you scared and brokenhearted. But if she's doing damage to herself and if you really love her (and I know you do), then get the proof and get some help.

That's pretty much where this chapter has to end. You and your family are going to need some face-to-face counseling that no book can provide.

As a man and the leader of your family, you may be tempted to try to fix the problem yourself. Having to seek professional help may even feel like you've somehow failed as a father. But just the opposite is true. Exposing dark corners of your home to the light of truth is a courageous act and requires strength and fearlessness most men don't have.

The Bible promises that our job is to shine God's truth on any and all dark secrets and he will do the rest. "Have nothing to do with the fruitless deeds of darkness, but rather expose them. It is shameful even to mention what the disobedient do in secret. But everything exposed by the light becomes visible—and everything that is illuminated becomes a light" (Ephesians 5:11-13).

You may want to make a few phone calls today. Get a recommendation from your pastor. Make sure any professional you bring in approaches the challenge from a biblical perspective.

If the time does come to confront the problem with professional help, expect it to be painful. Expect weeks or months of anger, denial, and separation. Expect to miss your little girl. Expect to have your own set of regrets and feelings of guilt. But also expect to walk through this dark storm and find healing on the other side.

Takeaway

Remember that your daughter trusts you. She trusts that you will do what needs to be done to protect her and provide for her.

"Be watchful, stand firm in the faith, act like men, be strong."
—1 CORINTHIANS 16:13 ESV

A Daughter Needs Her Dad...

To Know Who's on First

Every year, the third-, fourth-, and fifth-graders at Lincoln School in St. Charles, Illinois, put on a talent show. The teachers do a good job of encouraging students to participate even if they don't have a lot of talent. Rae Anne came home pretty excited about the whole deal and informed me that quite a few of the acts involved parents and kids performing together. She also informed me that she had already signed us up as a father–daughter act. What that act might be was totally up in the air.

Well, I don't sing or dance in public. At the time, Rae Anne had not yet learned how to juggle. I thought about sawing her in half, but my magic saw still had bloodstains from an earlier failed attempt. Rae would have made an excellent Cordelia to my King Lear, but a Shakespearean tragedy might have been a little deep for the elementary-school crowd.

As a father and daughter who appreciated wordplay, we'd already developed some pretty sweet comic timing practicing the arts of irony, parody, puns, knock-knock jokes, sarcasm, slapstick, and satire. And, of course, we loved baseball. So we settled on a complete word-for-word reenactment of the classic Abbott and Costello routine "Who's on First?"

Rae Anne and I listened to a scratchy old recording of the bit and transcribed it word for word. Because of the repetition of the lines, the memorization wasn't easy. But we had it down cold. To refresh your memory, here's a short excerpt. Rae Anne played the reporter. I played the coach:

> Rae: That's what I want to find out. I want you to tell me the names of the fellows on the team.

Dad: I'm telling you. Who's on first, What's on second, I Don't Know is on third—

Rae: You know the fellows' names?

Dad: Yes.

Rae: Well, then who's playing first?

Dad: Yes.

Rae: I mean the fellow's name on first base.

Dad: Who.

Rae: The fellow playin' first base.

Dad: Who.

Rae: The guy on first base.

Dad: Who is on first.

Rae: Well, what are you askin' me for?

Dad: I'm not asking you—I'm telling you. Who is on first.

Rae: I'm asking you—who's on first?

Dad: That's the man's name.

Rae: That's who's name?

Dad: Yes.

As you may or may not recall, the outfielders are Why, Because, and Nobody, the pitcher and catcher are Tomorrow and Today, and the shortstop is I-don't-give-a-darn.

The afternoon of the talent show, the Lincoln School gym was packed with parents, staff, and every student in the school. There were some 30 acts. Rae and I were scheduled to perform number 20 or so.

As the first dozen acts unfolded, three things became very apparent. Lots of kids in our town were taking piano lessons—some explored the keys impressively, while some could barely plink out "Twinkle, Twinkle, Little Star." Secondly, in 2003 there was no shame in lip-syncing to

Britney Spears. I think we heard "Oops! I Did it Again" so many times that it was no longer ironic. And third, no other moms or dads were making an appearance on that stage.

I had been duped. Rae Anne insisted that other classmates had invited their parents' participation. Apparently those moms and dads were all smart enough to decline the offer.

The good news is that when our number came up, the crowd was eager for something completely different. And we gave it to them. Our comedic timing was impeccable. The laughs came early and often. We fluffed one or two lines, but no one noticed. The applause was long and sincere. More than a decade later, I still get stopped in the grocery store by parents and teachers who remember our performance.

To be clear, this was not the beginning of a father–daughter act that toured the countryside. Thinking back, Rae Anne and I have not shared a stage since then. Really, it was simply a daughter asking a dad to do something fun and a little risky. And a dad who accepted the challenge and tried to make it special.

Rae and Jay were the highlight of the afternoon. And, I believe all the other dads in the Lincoln School gym were just a little bit jealous.

Takeaway

When your daughter invites you to do anything, do it. Drop what you're doing. Rearrange your schedule. Make her request to spend time with her daddy your biggest priority. This may be the only time she asks.

> *"The duty of comedy is to correct men by amusing them."*
>
> —MOLIERE

A Daughter Needs Her Dad…

To Rig a Handle on Her Surfboard

It's crazy how many movies are about fathers and their kids.

Movies about fathers and sons tend to be about how the son is trying to live up to the expectations of his aloof, demanding, or deceased father. Several examples come to mind. *Superman. Field of Dreams. Top Gun. The Lion King. October Sky. Elf. Dead Poet's Society. It's a Wonderful Life. Star Wars.* These movies all feature a young man (or creature) who endures an internal struggle deciding whether or not he should follow or abandon his father's footsteps.

Movies about dads and daughters, on the other hand, seem to be about fathers having trouble letting go of their little girl. The turning point of those films occurs when the father realizes that his daughter is not abandoning him, but actually still needs him in her life. There's usually a pivotal scene in which the dad gets one more chance to do something for his daughter that helps her find a new strength and actually venture forth on her own terms. Consider the father–daughter conflict in these movies. *Father of the Bride. Dirty Dancing. The Little Mermaid. Pocahontas. Fiddler on the Roof. To Kill a Mockingbird. Fly Away Home. Pride and Prejudice. The Vow. Trouble with the Curve. Paper Moon. Armageddon. On Golden Pond.*

In case you didn't realize it, Hollywood is in the business of making money. And they are well aware that conflict between fathers and their offspring is a universal touch point that sells tickets. Can't you hear King Triton shouting, "Ariel!" or Tevye singing, "When did she get to be a beauty?" Or even Patrick Swayze telling the father of Jennifer Grey's character, "Nobody puts Baby in a corner."

Speaking of films, have you seen *Soul Surfer*? If not, do yourself a favor and sit down with your daughter (or entire family) and take it in. It's the true story of Bethany Hamilton, an up-and-coming competitive surfer who loses an arm in a shark attack. Yet she courageously overcomes all odds to become a champion once again. The location and production draw you in. Dennis Quaid and Helen Hunt are well cast as Bethany's dad and mom. Even Carrie Underwood adds an inspired cameo as a youth pastor. Thankfully, the producers stayed faithful to the core motivations of Bethany and her family. There's a clear Christian message present, without the movie turning corny, fake, or over-the-top. It's nicely done.

When asked, "What's the movie about?" most casual film viewers would rattle off a quick review sounding very much like the above paragraph. But, like quite a few movies (including the 20 or so mentioned previously), *Soul Surfer* is about a father and his coming-of-age child. The telltale scene occurs in the movie's final reel, after Bethany comes full circle and realizes she can't give up on God's plan for her life. She wants and needs to surf. Unfortunately, there's a maneuver she can't do with just one arm. Surfers paddling out and looking for the next perfect wave need to "duck dive" under lesser waves. In the scene, Bethany has realized it's just too hard for her to stay on her surfboard. So the teenager walks across the sand to her father's outdoor work shack and says the words that every father loves to hear:

"*Dad, I need your help.*"

"*Name it.*"

"*I think I want to compete.*"

"*You sure? You don't have to, you know.*"

"*I'll take it heat by heat.*"

"*Okay.*"

"*So, Dad, we need to figure out something. Some way that when I duck dive, I don't get pounded.*"

That's when the dad reaches up to the rafters and pulls down a secret weapon he has already designed and built for his daughter. A surfboard with a sturdy rope handle she can grip when she needs to dive below water.

Dennis Quaid's character smiles, shows off his thoughtfully-designed invention, and offers a matter-of-fact reply to his daughter—who is surprised, but not really.

"You mean something like this?"

"Yeah."

With that turning point established, the screen cuts to a visual of a giant wave and a flourish of dramatic music as Bethany, equipped with trusting faith and a flourish of confidence in God's call, puts her new customized surfboard to the test. All of that leads to a soul-satisfying ending to the film. Again, it's all a true story and well worth a couple hours with your family. The credits roll accompanied by astonishing sequences of the real Bethany dominating giant waves.

The obvious lesson, of course, is about perseverance and overcoming challenges. But it was more than that. It's an unmistakable lesson about the power and responsibility of fathers—you, me, and our heavenly Father.

Bethany's dad knew his daughter so well that he knew what she needed even before she did. He had assessed her need, worked out the solution in advance, and was ready to present it. All Bethany had to do was ask.

"Dad, I need your help."

"You mean something like this?"

She asked. He answered. And her exact needs are met. From what I understand about God's nature, that's pretty much how prayer works. In the early pages of the New Testament, right before teaching the Lord's Prayer to the disciples, Jesus explains to them that when you pray, "your Father knows what you need before you ask him" (Matthew 6:8).

Likewise, a devoted earthly father should know his children so well that he might get a handle on what they need before they need it. When that happens, despite impossible odds, dreams often do come true. Just like in the movies.

Takeaway

What is your daughter struggling with right now? Do you know? You should. On your own, in secret, see if you can figure out a solution to that problem. Don't force it on her or fix everything for her. If she works it out on her own, that's great. But if she comes to you and says, "Dad, I need your help," you need to be ready with some fresh ideas, possible solutions, and maybe a customized surfboard.

> *"I tell you, whatever you ask for in prayer, believe*
> *that you have received it, and it will be yours."*
>
> —Jesus, in Mark 11:24

A Daughter Needs Her Dad...

To Tweak Your Coaching Style

Dads who were stud athletes back in high school (like you) make great coaches for their daughter's sports teams years later.

You know the thrill of victory and the agony of defeat. You know that practice makes perfect. You know what it means to give 110 percent. You know how to shake off a bad play to get ready for the next play. You know there's no "I" in team, but you also recognize that games are won by outstanding individual performances. You know coaching is more than X's and O's. You know coaching is about getting players to reach inside themselves to give more than they ever thought possible.

But what you might not know is that coaching boys is different than coaching girls.

"What?" you say. "Boy athletes are different than girl athletes?"

Yes, they are. But we're not talking about things like competitiveness, athleticism, strength, and endurance. In high-school and college sports, you really can't differentiate between boys and girls in those areas. Today's young female athletes are most certainly competitive, athletic, strong, and enduring.

On a case-by-case basis, you can find examples when girls take their sports less seriously. And yes, the men's record for high jump, shot put, and the 40-yard dash will always be higher, farther, and faster than the women's record.

But let's all agree that girl athletes—in many ways—have the same dedication and commitment as the boys.

Still, there are differences. And if you're coaching your daughter's team, some of these differences might take you by surprise.

A disclaimer is in order at this point. This list is not scientific or quantifiable. It may sound a little sexist. But if you ask for an honest answer from an experienced coach, he or she will confirm that teams of girls often exhibit a social and emotional aspect that is quite different than teams of boys.

- Boys understand the pecking order. A boy sitting on the bench at the tip-off of a basketball game is more likely to accept the idea that the five starters are better than him. A girl nonstarter will hold a grudge against the coach or the player who "stole" her spot, while a boy will work harder in practice to earn a starting spot.

- Girls care about how they look in their uniform. Boys like a sharp logo and judge new uniforms on how they feel. Girls don't like pants that make their behinds look big.

- On every girls' team, at least two of the girls will hate each other. During a basketball game, one girl may literally never pass the ball to her teammate because of their animosity. Boys won't let feelings impact the game.

- If a teammate is a jerk or loudmouth, the boys will accept him if he plays hard and makes the team better. With girls, the team chemistry will dissolve and losses will pile up.

- Boys have pregame rituals. Girls sing in the dugout.

- A girl pitcher may cry right on the mound when she gets taken out of the game. A boy pitcher waits until he's six feet from the dugout and then chucks his glove at the water cooler.

- When a coach directly confronts a boy about missing a pick, not tagging up on a deep fly ball, or some other neglected strategy, the boy will get mad at himself and remember the lesson. A girl thinks it's a personal attack by the coach and may miss the lesson entirely.

- Girls often play sports for the social aspect during the game. Boys play sports to play sports. The social aspect comes after—hours, days, and years later.

- A girl will efficiently shake off a tough loss and move to the next scheduled event in her busy social life. A boy will replay the turning points of the game in his head—taking much of the blame upon himself.

None of the above is an absolute. And as the level of competition elevates, the differences between male and female athletes typically diminish. Still, dads need to coach young female athletes with a different set of expectations. You should certainly expect the girls on your team to work hard, dig deep, compete with determination, and listen intently to your pep talks and bull sessions. But also expect them to bring a different set of priorities and respond to your coaching with a different batch of emotions.

Unfortunately, one thing isn't so different. With this new generation of fierce and dedicated female athletes comes a new set of parents who are just as obnoxious, maybe even more so, when they root for their daughter. Good luck, coach.

Takeaway

Despite the frightening scenario described above, go ahead and volunteer to coach or assist with your young daughter's soccer, basketball, or softball team. Your daughter will discover an entire new set of skills and gifts that will serve her well in many life pursuits, including leadership, determination, perseverance, and athletic prowess. And you'll be right there to see it.

"My dad was my backbone throughout my career. He was the one who spent the hours on the bucket catching my pitches."

—Jennie Finch

A Daughter Needs Her Dad...

To Make Her Wishes Come True

This is going to be a hard chapter to read for some dads. And I apologize for that. If a dad is truly raising his kids with his best effort, the last thing I want to do is make him feel guilty.

As I speak with men's groups around the country, the topic of fathering draws a diverse crowd. I'm still surprised at how many guys show up who are in their sixties. After the event, almost every time, one of those older men comes up to me and says something like "I sure wish I would have heard this talk twenty years ago while my kids were still at home." Their attitude is appreciation for the message I'm bringing to dads in the trenches. But the distant look in their eyes suggests a loss that makes me sad.

Any statement that begins "I wish..." usually has an undercurrent of new potential or lost opportunity.

When your child says, "I wish..." you have the perfect opening to say, "Wow! That would be great. How can I help you make that wish come true?" When an older person says, "I wish..." it's typically a regret.

Below is a list of statements made by older girls and young women when asked to think about their fathers and come up with a statement that began with those two words: "I wish." Some of these are exact quotes. Some are paraphrases.

"I wish my father would have kept his promises."

"I wish my father would have cared about my volleyball games as much as he cared about my brother's basketball games."

"I wish I hadn't been so hard to live with as a teenager. We didn't exactly get along and it was mostly my fault."

"When a boy came to pick me up on a date when I was 16 years old, I wish my dad would have been the kind of guy who met him at the door with a shotgun saying, 'Don't mess with my daughter or I'll mess with you.'"

"I wish my dad would have quit smoking."

"I wish my father had asked someone for help. He was messed up."

"I wish my father had sat beside me listening to albums instead of walking past my room and telling me how bad the music was."

"I use to lock myself in my bedroom and sometimes I would sit there and hope that my dad would break down the door and tell me he loved me and that everything would be okay."

"I wish my dad and mom had never met."

"I wish my daddy was still alive so he could see what I'm doing now and he could tell me he was proud of me."

"I wish my dad would have taught me how to be different."

"I wish my daddy would have been there to protect me in college."

"I wish my dad was here so I could dance with him again."

"I wish I would have met my father."

"I wish my daddy still tucked me in at night. He stopped doing it when we moved to Bloomington. I was nine."

"I wish my dad was here because he would have made an awesome grampa."

"I wish all kids had a dad like my dad. Most of my friends can barely talk to their dads."

Looking at the above list leads me to three thoughts.

First, none of us are perfect. All of us have had moments and seasons in which we were not at our fathering best. So cut yourself some slack.

Second, make sure your daughter loves God and is pursuing his call in her life. That will ensure that all the good stuff and even all the crud that happens will somehow—in God's timing—be turned into a long-term positive experience. The Bible teaches, "We know that God causes everything to work together for the good of those who love God and are called according to his purpose for them" (Romans 8:28 NLT). That's a truth you can trust. That's a promise that helps you and your daughter live with no regrets. God can and will turn darkness to light.

Third, if you dare, go ahead and ask your own daughter to make an "I wish" statement. Maybe a bunch of them. Let her know you want to know her hopes and dreams. Expect her first round of wishes to be for a puppy, a pony, or a Porsche. But then ask her to wish for something related to you and her. You will very likely get a short list of things that are quite possible. Things you can do and places you can go together. Write them on your heart. And see what you can do to make her simple wishes come true. Or did you need an excuse to buy that Porsche?

Takeaway

God gave daddies to little girls to make wishes come true. Although, not necessarily the wishes she wishes for.

> *"What makes the difference between wishing and realizing our wishes? Lots of things, and it may take months or years for a wish to come true, but it's far more likely to happen when you care so much about a wish that you'll do all you can to make it happen."*
>
> —FRED ROGERS

A Daughter Needs Her Dad...

To Untangle Cultural Expectations

One of the primary goals with all our children—boys and girls—is to help them find their God-given strengths and use them to serve him. In other words, help them be who God wants them to be.

For a son, it's still pretty straightforward. Maximize his abilities in athletics and academics. Insist he engage in some artistic pursuit such as music, sculpture, painting, photography, or theater. Plug him in at church. And then help him find one or two additional challenging activities that fit his personality, like debate, speech, filmmaking, software or web design, sports medicine, chess, poetry, journalism, stand-up comedy, biblical studies, astronomy, and so on. Since there literally isn't enough time to do it all, he will choose to drop some of these interests one by one. When the dust settles, bam! Your son is left with some valuable experiences and revealed talents that will lead to a successful career and an ever-so-happy life.

With girls, it's not so easy. Women have to do all of the above and battle cultural expectations the entire time.

And what are those cultural expectations? They may not be what you think. There is no longer an assumption that women will find personal fulfillment staying home, cooking dinner, and making babies. Actually, it's just about the opposite.

The culture has saddled bright young women—like your daughter—with a long list of crushing expectations that are virtually impossible to live up to. According to the push and pull of today's societal norms, your daughter has to achieve at a higher level than her male peers in every statistical category and look good doing it. Hair and makeup just right. Skinny. And always with a smile on her face.

I would call it an impossible task, but today's young women seem to be doing it. Since 2000, women have represented about 57 percent of enrollments at U.S. colleges. Women today earn 53 percent of all doctoral degrees. Since 1990, the number of women CEOs of Fortune 500 companies has increased by 600 percent.[7]

Furthermore, today's women are leading the way in these educational and professional advancements while giving allegiance to the impossible standards of beauty established by the 230-billion-dollar cosmetics industry.[8]

The unavoidable conclusion is this: Your daughter needs to be brilliant and look fabulous. *Or does she?*

Is your daughter required to meet the burdensome pronouncements of today's culture? If God wired her to be a corporate tycoon, Olympic champion, presidential hopeful, or Academy Award–winning actress, that's awesome. Come alongside her and cheer her on.

But just as awesome is the idea that the plan for her life is far different from the expectations established by today's culture. No matter what, you need to be proud of her. Today and decades from now, she is going to be making many of her decisions based on the idea of what her dad might think.

What if her strengths and gifts lead her to be a stay-at-home mom for 30 years and then run for city council? What if God is calling her to hold and nurture babies in an orphanage in Uganda? What if she's called to be a special-education teacher? Or put her own life on hold as she becomes the prime caregiver for an aging mother-in-law? Those are the recent life scenarios embraced by my wife, niece, daughter-in-law, and sister-in-law. Believe me, there's real purpose and a sense of satisfaction in all those pursuits.

So don't let your daughter submit blindly to the expectations of the world. And don't you, Dad, burden your little girl with any of your own unequivocal paternal expectations...except one.

Go back to the premise with which we began this chapter. The one expectation you should convey with love and humility to your blossoming daughter is that she should trust God and seek his will. Psalm 37 says it well: "Commit your way to the LORD; trust in him and he will do this: He will make your righteous reward shine like the dawn, your vindication like the noonday sun" (Psalm 37:5-6).

Walking in the way of the Lord. Shining like the dawn. For your daughter, that's a brilliant and fabulous existence that will last for eternity.

Takeaway

Your daughter is going to face these cultural pressures earlier than you think. She'll be sitting in a middle-school classroom, look around, and think she has already fallen behind in school, sports, fashion, and physical appearance. Without minimizing her feelings, let her know that God is proud of who she is and has wonderful things prepared for her. Remind her also that you're her biggest fan.

> *"What does the LORD your God ask of you but to fear the LORD your God, to walk in obedience to him, to love him, to serve the LORD your God with all your heart and with all your soul, and to observe the LORD's commands and decrees that I am giving you today for your own good?"*
>
> —DEUTERONOMY 10:12-13

A Daughter Needs Her Dad…

To Say a Few Things So Many Times That She Repeats Them Before You Finish Talking

My daughter and I have a running joke. Except it's not a joke at all. It was inspired by a children's book by John Trent. The following is a transcript of how that conversation might have gone the first time I said it.

"Ya know, Rae-ster, I've been thinking."

"What, Daddy?" (As she hangs on my every word.)

"This is kind of crazy, but I've been thinking…I've been thinking that if they took all the six-year-old girls in the entire world and put them in one long line…I would choose…you!" (Her wide-eyed smile is followed by a tremendous hug.)

Little girls need to hear that kind of thing. When a dad says, "I'd choose you," he's not saying his daughter is perfect or never makes mistakes. He's just saying that he's glad she exists and that he enjoys spending time with her. It's a confirmation of unconditional love. Dad might trade in his car or change jobs, but that daddy–daughter bond is unbreakable. In her first-grade class, Chelsea may be taller, Becky may be smarter, and Sophia may be prettier, but she has heard it from his own mouth. *Daddy would choose me.*

After we'd had a similar dialogue more than a dozen times during the grammar-school years, the rhythm of the conversation changed, but the message was still the same.

"Hey, Rae, I've been thinking."

"What, Dad?"

"If they lined up all the nine-year-old girls in the whole world..."

"What would you do, Dad?" (Said with a slight smile and slight sigh.)

"I'd choose you."

"Good to know, Dad." (Said with a hint of sarcasm.)

Over the next few years slight variations on the theme emerge.

"Hey, Rae Anne, I've been thinking." (No response.) *"If they lined up all the 12-year-old girls in the..."*

"If they lined up all the 12-year-old girls in the whole world, you'd choose me. Got it, Dad. Check. Thanks." (Said with a thicker slice of sarcasm.)

Here's one of my favorite variations.

"Hey, Rae, I've been thinking."

"Tell me, Dad. I'm setting aside my algebra homework to hear exactly what you've been thinking." (She doesn't even look up.)

"If they lined up all the 15-year-old girls in the whole world..."

"You'd choose me."

"No, actually I'd choose Ally. She's a good daughter and uses slightly less sarcasm."

(After a pause) *"Good choice. Ally is a much better daughter than I will ever be. Let me know how that works out for you."*

Ally, as you might suspect, has been Rae Anne's best friend since they were toddlers. And, of course, I'm not proud that Rae Anne uses quite as much sarcasm as she does. I just wish I knew where she learned it. I'd strangle the scoundrel.

Anyway. Dad, when you find a phrase of encouragement or unconditional love that works, go ahead and say it loud and clear until it becomes second nature to your daughter. When she faces a challenge to your family's core values, your words are going to echo in her head.

After years of bantering, I know that if Rae Anne is ever feeling undervalued or out of the loop, a small part of her says, "That's okay. I know my dad would choose me." And that may happen when I'm on the other side of the planet.

Over the years, I've heard and sometimes used a few other phrases that you might want to say three or four times (or maybe a thousand times) to your daughter. When she starts repeating them back to you, you'll know your voice is in her head. As long as it's a positive statement, that's a good thing. Try these out:

"You know, the choices they're making on this show…there are better options."

"When you wear something like that…it sends a message to boys you don't want to send."

"The easiest way to do well in college…is to go to class."

"I understand your dilemma. You do what you need to do…but just remember there are some things you can't undo."

"The culture has made it a joke, but it's still a good idea to ask…what would Jesus do?"

"Yes, you can absolutely borrow my [specify item here], but when you're finished…put it back where it belongs."

Feel free to come up with some of your own. Actually, you probably already have some. Be warned: None of these should come off as nagging. (Real men don't nag.) They should sound like new thoughts every time you use them. If they cause an eye roll or deep sigh, that's okay. That means they heard you. If you can say the first part and they finish your thought by speaking the last part, then you're in sync. If they say, "I know, I know…" then feel free to add one more line. Maybe something like:

"You know? I'm glad to know you know. That means I'm doing my job."

Takeaway

Sarcasm is a dangerous tool for dads. A little goes a long way. But you're so smart, you already knew that, right?

"What I tell you three times is true."

—Lewis Carroll

A Daughter Needs Her Dad…

To Be Overjoyed She's a Girl

The year was 1993. My family was approaching near-legendary status in the neighborhood. Rita and I already had four amazing sons ages 4 to 12. Alec, Randy, Max, and Isaac. Neighbors were beginning to describe our place as the "house with all the boys." Best of all, I was the ringleader. There was always someone playing catch in the side yard or touch football in the street or inventing a new game with ever-changing rules on the driveway. Rita and I were building men who would surely do great things.

In March, kid number five was due. And since we had proven ourselves faithful with four boys, it was assumed that number five would be no different.

Truth be told, I was hoping for a girl. I was having so much fun bonding with my sons that I was sure Rita wanted and needed to do the same thing with a daughter. And for me, a little girl would be someone I could spoil, have tea parties with, kiss on the forehead, dance with, and walk down the aisle someday. My brother had three daughters, and there was something about his relationship with them that left me a little jealous. I loved my boys, but a daughter would surely be the icing on the cake.

Pregnant couples talk, of course. And Rita was pretty clear that she wanted a boy, mostly because she was confident in her proven ability to raise sons. I couldn't argue. They had not yet hit the teenage years, but so far the boys were turning out pretty well. The four of them were delivering just the right amount of roughhousing, tree-climbing, and tracking mud through the house. It was all very entertaining. Twenty years later, I can quote my wife exactly: "I know how to do boys. Boys I can do. Girls are harder. I was a girl once and I know. I wouldn't want to have to raise me."

Now I happen to think that Rita turned out pretty well. And the idea of a little girl growing up to be a slightly taller replica of my beautiful bride seemed like a good idea. Rita's insistence on delivering us a fifth son only confirmed my desire to be a dad to a daughter.

And I won. On March 12, 1993, Rita Anne gave birth to our perfect Rae Anne. (For the record, the delivery was VBA3C. Ask your wife—or check it online—if you don't understand that bit of medical wizardry.)

Like the birth of all my other kids, holding Rae Anne brought a mixture of emotions. Wonder. Bewilderment. Relief. Humbleness. Honor. Love. New responsibility.

In the weeks to follow, well-wishers would offer a variety of light-hearted sentiments, all containing a grain of truth. "Congratulations! You finally got your girl." "What are you going to do? You don't know anything about little girls!" "You are in for a shocker. Girls are so different than boys." "With all those older brothers, I feel sorry for any boy that comes to the door asking for a date."

One of my favorite quips came from sports-minded friends: "A girl? After four boys? Well, I guess you didn't get your basketball team." The punch line of that joke is that years later Rae Anne was my only child to play varsity high-school basketball. The boys were all wrestlers.

So that's my story. Four boys and a girl. And I'm glad. Each one different. Each one God picked out for Rita and me. That's just the way it works.

Finally, this chapter needs to end with one serious warning. And one delightful surprise.

First, don't ever…ever…allow your daughter to believe for one second that you were disappointed she was a girl. I know it's too late for some of you—that unfortunate idea has already slipped out. Even if it wasn't really true, the thought may have presented itself and found its way out of your insensitive speaking orifice. If that's the case, then this very moment commit the next five decades of your life to loving your little girl for the person she is. Unconditionally. Relentlessly. (And the same goes for any dad who had a boy and wanted a girl.)

And the surprise is this. If you pour your heart into your daughter, stay connected with her, and model a healthy marriage for her, there's a real good chance one day soon she's going to repeat the pattern you established. In other words, your daughter is going to provide you with a son-in-law. What's even a little more surprising—and a little frightening—is that your new son-in-law may reflect many of your own personal character traits. Which makes perfect sense. After all, for two decades or more you will have been dating your daughter and treating her exactly the way you expect her future husband to treat her.

And then there's the matter of grandsons and granddaughters. But we'll save that for another book.

Takeaway

Imagine your father saying to you, "Son, you bring me so much joy. More than I could ever deserve." Would that make your day? Your week? Your year? Well, Dad, fashion a similar statement and speak it out loud to your daughter. And make her day, today.

> *"There are two kinds of fathers in traditional households: the*
> *fathers of sons and the fathers of daughters. These two kinds of*
> *fathers sometimes co-exist in one and the same man. For instance,*
> *Daughter's Father kisses his little girl goodnight, strokes her hair,*
> *hugs her warmly, then goes into the next room where he becomes*
> *Son's Father, who says in a hearty voice, perhaps with a light punch*
> *on the boy's shoulder: 'Goodnight, Son, see ya in the morning.'"*
>
> —LETTY COTTIN POGREBIN

A Daughter Needs Her Dad...

To Live with Dents

High-school sophomore Rae Anne had her driver's license, but no car. Which was perfectly fine. She didn't drive herself to school every day like many of her friends, but with three vehicles in the driveway and four drivers in the household, there was usually one she could grab after school or on weekends. Rae always asked permission before taking a car and even pumped in a few dollars of gas once in a while.

The system worked. Until she cut the angle too close pulling into a high-school parking spot, denting the front bumper on my car and the back fender of the car belonging to one of the boys on the golf team. She called me right away, and I drove my wife's car to the school parking lot. Without emotion, I surveyed the damage. Rae Anne had probably been traveling about two miles per hour, but it doesn't take much to dent today's plastic bumpers. She simply didn't have the experience to maneuver into the narrow parking spots at our high school and was likely too embarrassed to back up and try to get a better angle. I estimated the damage at $800 for each car. I wasn't far off.

Rae Anne left a note on the golfer's car, and I left any repercussions, consequences, and punishments for later. Actually, there was no punishment. After all, it was an accident. But there was a consequence. Just about all of Rae Anne's life savings went to the body shop that repaired the golfer's car. (He was very grateful for the note left on his windshield, by the way.)

As for the four-year-old dent on the fender of my eight-year-old

Chevy? It's still there. Rae Anne couldn't afford to fix it. I have a high deductible so it would have made no sense to go to our insurance company. And if I would have paid for the dent out of my own pocket, that would have essentially told my daughter that dents go away miraculously. So, there it remains.

At first I was embarrassed driving a car with an obvious pucker on the front bumper. But before long the dent became a daily reminder. A reminder that stuff doesn't matter. A reminder that the outcome of my daughter's first accident was a lesson, not an injury. (It could have been much worse.) And a reminder that Rae Anne knew she could call her daddy when something bad happened.

For most of my adult life, I've carried a monthly car payment. But my old Chevy has been paid off for more than four years and it feels kind of nice. I have a mechanic I trust and a car that starts in the morning. I may just drive it another 100,000 miles.

Takeaway

You want your daughter to call you when something bad happens. As you help sort out the mess, use it as a connection point to bring you closer together in the long run. Don't pile on, because that always makes a bad situation worse. On the other hand, don't make the problem magically disappear. Hold her responsible, but take enough of the burden on yourself so she doesn't get crushed. Make sense?

> *"Now that women are jockeys, baseball umpires, atomic scientists, and business executives, maybe someday they can master parallel parking."*
>
> —Bill Vaughn

A Daughter Needs Her Dad…

To Help Her Build a Lemonade Stand (Metaphorically)

The adage is true—life gives out lemons. To you. And to everyone else, including your daughter.

Without asking, I know what you want for her. Out loud you might say, "I pray for my daughter to be happy and fulfill God's plan for her life." That's nice and honorable. But your unspoken thoughts want something closer to perfection. You imagine your little girl will be a well-recognized scholar/athlete/leader through high school, graduate college in four years with an impressive degree, get married to someone just like you in her twenties, give you three perfect grandchildren in her thirties, build a dream house just a few miles away from yours, and stay happily married for the rest of her life.

I have no statistics to back this up, but that "perfect" scenario probably happens to less than one-tenth of one percent of all girls.

Taking it one step further. Dad, if you start expressing those thoughts to your daughter, you might be saddling her with a list of impossible standards and expectations that drives her away and leaves her feeling like a permanent failure. She values your approval. It's quite possible that she wants to meet a man like you and build a family like the one in which she grew up. But that has to come out of her gifts, goals, and dreams. Not yours.

When a dad puts his daughter on a track of specific expectations, there's a high likelihood that an unexpected jolt of reality will take her off that track. We live in a fallen world in which sin, disease, abuse, accidents, discrimination, mental illness, materialism, deceit, and a long list of other nasty things lurk just around the next corner. We don't need to look for explanations or excuses. Sometimes suffering happens as a direct result of our bad choices. Sometimes bad things just happen.

If you've already painted the impossible perfect scenario for how your daughter's life will look, that canvas should be taken down off the wall before anyone sees it. Especially her.

What happens when she gets cut from a team or doesn't get into the college of her choice? What happens when one bad choice leaves her unmarried and pregnant? What happens when she and her husband can't get pregnant? Or a child has Downs? Or her husband turns abusive? When illness, accident, or some seemingly random series of events leaves a gaping wound in her heart, mind, or soul, will you still be her champion?

When life gives her lemons, your daughter needs her dad to help build a lemonade stand. There may be other people in her life that love her almost as much as you. But you're the one who has dreamed about her future since before she was even born. You see how the pieces fit. You know how to take the bad stuff and help turn it somehow into good stuff.

Like so many points in the book, this concept is another in which earthly fathers can follow the example of our heavenly Father. Listen to how the Bible explains the process God uses to turn negatives into positives.

> We boast in the hope of the glory of God. Not only so, but we also glory in our sufferings, because we know that suffering produces perseverance; perseverance, character; and character, hope. And hope does not put us to shame, because God's love has been poured out into our hearts through the Holy Spirit, who has been given to us (Romans 5:2-5).

Don't eagerly open the door to sin and suffering. Don't be indifferent to what's going on in your daughter's life because you expect failure. Keep setting high expectations. But don't be taken by surprise when your expectations fall short. Stuff happens. When the issues are eternal, teach your daughter to count on hope through the Holy Spirit. When the issues require human hands to be involved, raise yours. Be the hero with the hammer to build that lemonade stand.

Teach your daughter to squeeze every drop out of every lemon and add just the right amount of sugar, and stand beside her as she enjoys some ice-cold refreshment. Don't forget to say thanks when she shares a glass with you. Don't be surprised when she also offers a glass to others she meets on the road of life.

Takeaway

It's quite a balancing act. Pushing our kids to reach for the stars. And being there to catch them when they fall. One more reason God made dads with strong arms and strong hearts.

"This is the very perfection of a man, to find out his own imperfections."

—AUGUSTINE

A Daughter Needs Her Dad…

To Help Her Build a Lemonade Stand (Literally)

The last chapter may have felt like a bit of a challenge, so maybe it's time to head a different direction. How about if we brainstorm some business ideas for your daughter who's between the ages of 8 and 15? Hopefully, this list will unleash some of your own creativity while also helping you inspire some innovation and business savvy in your young daughter.

Lemonade stand. This classic American roadside attraction needs to stay classic. Despite the title of this chapter, the lemonade stand doesn't have to be constructed of framing lumber and plywood. A card table, chairs, and tablecloth are all she really needs. But if you want to get out the tool belt and Skilsaw, that's totally your call. No matter what, your daughter has to design and post a hand-lettered sign that says "Lemonade 25¢" or whatever she decides to charge. Also, she doesn't have to bother with real lemons, but the product has to be served ice-cold. Do a safety check. Pick a nice warm day. And it's really okay if she drinks all the profits.

Dog-sitting. This is a big responsibility, but a much appreciated service around any neighborhood. When the canine member of a family is stuck at home for a long day or several days, the dog owner needs to know that their pooch is not on the loose. Safety for gal and pup are the biggest priority. So make sure a grown-up monitors the first couple visits so the job (and the dog) is not too big. Ask the dog owner to write down all instructions. And don't be surprised by anything that might happen with a cooped-up canine.

Cat-sitting. This is easy. Except sometimes the cat might hide under a table, on a shelf, or behind a sofa. Ask the owner ahead of time what to do if you can't find old Felix. On second thought, why bother? It's a cat! Who really cares about cats?

Dog-walking. Dog-washing. Dog doo duty. If your daughter loves the neighborhood spaniel or beagle, to a ten-year-old girl this is like getting paid for doing something you would do for free. Except for the doo-doo part.

Lawn-mowing. Not just a job for boys, but insist she practices for two or three seasons on your lawn before soliciting work from the neighbors. Pretty sneaky, huh?

Babysitting. Some towns have local ordinances about ages, but girls can usually begin sitting at about 13. I've heard reports that good teenage baby-sitters are making up to a whopping $15 per hour. Your local park district may have certification classes.

Mommy's helper. Moms who work out of their homes or have busy sched-ules sometimes hire middle-school girls to come over a few hours a day during the summer just to keep their kids safe and busy. Everyone wins.

Weed-pulling. This might be a gardener's assistant job. Any neighbor who does their own yard work might love to have your sweet daughter's companionship for an hour here or there. For a fee, of course.

Candy striper. Many hospitals and nursing homes still invite young teens to volunteer around the building. In the gift shop or reception area—clean-ing, filing, delivering lab specimens, and interacting with patients and staff. A great idea for a daughter who may be considering a career in medicine.

Leaf-raking. Snow-shoveling. After your family shovels or rakes your own yard together, send your daughter on a mission. Have her ring doorbells with a rake or shovel in her hand. When the homeowner asks how much, she just has to say, "Whatever you think is fair." Thoroughness counts, so check on her to see how she's doing. Maybe bring her a bottle of water or hot cocoa.

It's a thought-provoking list. You and your daughter could probably add your own ideas, depending on your part of the world. From pool-cleaning to corn-detasseling to clam-digging. But of course, the point of all these income opportunities is not income at all. It's all about finding one more excuse to plot and plan with your daughter. It's about helping her explore her world and open herself to the possibilities out there and within herself. It's about giving her new responsibilities while you're still around to help with any crisis management large and small.

The benefits extend further than you might imagine. Pocket money. Job skills. References. New friends. Ministry opportunities. Stuff to include on college applications. Overcoming shyness. Business savvy. Confidence. The ability to take directions from a boss. And a new understanding of how the world works. Too many kids these days head into adulthood without some of these basic life concepts.

Early work experience will give your daughter appreciation for the value of a buck. And an eye-opening understanding of why you're gone 50-plus hours a week. Plus, she'll finally understand why sometimes you come home from work in a mood that says, "I've had a tough day."

Takeaway

The best way to get your daughter self-motivated might be to share stories from when you were her age. Delivering newspapers. Cutting lawns. Bussing tables. Or regretting all the time you spent playing Pac-Man or Super Mario.

*"The plans of the diligent lead to profit as
surely as haste leads to poverty."*

—Proverbs 21:5

A Daughter Needs Her Dad…

To Not Blame Authors, Artists, Singers, and Movie Producers

This is one of those chapters that may get me in trouble. Because there really is a ton of garbage out there—being produced in the name of art—and it would be really nice to have someone to blame.

A vast array of today's so-called "entertainment" is violent, depressing, graphic, filthy, angry, and devoid of hope. Plus, it seems like every generation sinks to a new level of what they consider acceptable in mainstream books, movies, art, and music. Even worse than the obvious assault on our senses may be the subtle systematic perversion of our worldview. In the name of tolerance, any choice made by anyone at any time is not to be judged.

But frankly, we shouldn't be surprised. The well-being of our daughters is not the responsibility of film studios, network executives, publishers, or music producers. They are just doing their job. Their assignment is to make as much money as possible for their companies. If they don't believe in God, why would they follow a biblical worldview when pushing their products to the marketplace?

With that in mind, Dad, I promise not to blame you for the garbage. Instead, I am challenging you to find a solution. Or at the very least, a solution when it comes to the well-being of your family. I think we all agree that it can't possibly be good for our daughters to fill their minds with garbage, lies, and half-truths.

The answer may be found in the passage of Scripture that reads,

"Brothers and sisters, whatever is true, whatever is noble, whatever is right, whatever is pure, whatever is lovely, whatever is admirable—if anything is excellent or praiseworthy—think about such things" (Philippians 4:8).

Does that sound like a plan? What if we all encouraged our daughters to open their hearts and minds only to things that are noble, pure, lovely, admirable, excellent, and praiseworthy?

Do such things exist? Certainly. But finding them takes work, research, and follow-through. A dad needs to read movie, music, and book reviews, talk to other parents, and be a student of the culture. We need to invest a little time and money to take our daughters to fine-art galleries and uplifting concerts. Seek out quality products from Christian artists and publishers, but also explore other resources as well.

Not so strangely, the human ability to create only exists because we were made in the image of the Creator. So even if the artist doesn't know it, God-inspired truth and beauty can hide in the corners of their creative works. Just be warned—even creative works that look harmless from afar can be dangerous. Innocent-looking art can often be even more dangerous than work that is labeled "For mature audiences only." The slope is slippery. Filmmakers especially can surprise audiences with disturbing themes that you won't see in their mainstream marketing campaign, but show up at the core of the film's message—a message you may not want your daughter to embrace.

Dads, we've got our work cut out for us. Teen-sex comedies and movies with themes of vampires, adultery, torture, and Satan worship still sell popcorn. Popular music continues to attract the teen-girl market, but lyrics from the new wave of female rockers are encouraging girls not to look for love, but look for sex without commitment. The hugely popular *Fifty Shades of Grey* trilogy has opened the floodgates to novels marketed to young women and teenage girls depicting lengthy and graphic sex scenes.

The easy answer is to censor everything. To blame the human creators of all this evil stuff and ask our government to make it all just go away. Phew. Wouldn't that be convenient?

A couple problems with that. First, it's not going to happen. Second, even if we could stop the professionals from creating things that reflect evil, evil would still exist. While here on earth, we cannot hope to eliminate evil. We can flee. We can warn others. We may even convert some of the professionals to our side. But from a father's perspective, our first order of business is to protect our young daughter from it. As she gets older, we can even equip her to battle against it.

So maybe the Bible passage above is the exact right place to start. First, help your daughter open her heart and mind to things worthy of praise. Then follow up with prayer that being exposed to such things will lead her to discover her own beauty. Which will give her confidence to create new art herself using her own gifts and passions, bringing her own personal radiance.

From my perspective, that sounds like a more effective strategy than blaming some executive sitting in an office in New York or Hollywood. Then suddenly, because of your daughter, some of the dark corners of the world will have a few less shadows.

Takeaway

Our daughters were created in the image of the Creator. Does your daughter know that? Does she know she also has the gift of creativity?

> *"There are a hundred men hacking at the branches of evil to every one who is striking at the roots of evil."*
>
> —HENRY WARD BEECHER

A Daughter Needs Her Dad...

To Extend His Pinky Properly at All Tea Parties

There's something magical about peeking out the kitchen window and seeing your young daughter interacting graciously, sincerely, and quite audibly with a table of inanimate party guests. Those guests may include a few stuffed bears, doggies, horsies, and bunnies, a Raggedy Ann, an American Girl doll, and the latest way-too-popular stuffed cartoon character of the week. If you have a good-natured golden retriever or basset hound, there's even a chance the young hostess has plopped them down at the table...where dog and daughter are engaged in very prim and proper conversation about the flight pattern of butterflies or the queen's upcoming visit.

How should you respond, Dad? I think you know. I think you need to follow your fathering instinct and do exactly what you want to do. Join her. Join the party. Even if she has not invited you, stroll out to the merry-making and ever-so-chivalrously make merry. Totally surrender to the fantasy and frivolity. Sit on the blanket, tiny picnic table, or doll furniture with your knees tucked up under your chin. Sip daintily. Stir counter-clockwise. Extend your pinky finger. Converse in polite tones with a slight British accent.

Little girls often create a fantasy world where all is well and only nice things happen. It's a perfectly appropriate and perfectly charming way to spend an afternoon. If only life would stay that way.

Part of your job, Dad, is to nurture that idyllic world for as long as possible. The media and culture are forcing little girls to grow up too fast too soon.

Following are a few examples of what you're up against.

Not long ago, Abercrombie & Fitch began marketing padded bras to seven-year-old girls. These garments apparently match the retailer's thong underwear collection with printed slogans such as "Kiss Me" and "Wink Wink." Dad, you may not want to even think about this, but according to one Beverly Hills salon owner, nearly 20 percent of the clients she sees for bikini waxes are 12 and under. *USA Today* reports that marketers are pushing girls as young as kindergarten into "premature adolescent rebellion." A proven merchandising strategy is to equip young girls to beg and cajole their parents until they give in. Marketers call it "pester power," and blindsided parents don't have a chance.[9]

My friend Dannah Gresh, author of *Six Ways to Keep the "Little" in Your Girl*, anticipated this looming challenge when her daughter Lexi was not yet in school. Thankfully, so did Dannah's husband, Bob. Starting with Lexi's fifth birthday, he helped his daughter stay in her little girl world with four carefully chosen gifts given through the years. The first was a heart-shaped pewter box with a blue-crystal bracelet. The box was engraved "To Lexi. From Daddy. Something Blue. December 28, 1998." Every five years Lexi received something from the wedding poem: "Something old. Something new. Something borrowed. Something blue." Pretty cool, right?

Watching her husband creatively and courageously enter into that girlish part of their daughter's world, Dannah says, he was actually "dreaming with her."[10] A dad dreaming with a daughter about growing up in the right time frame and with the right values will keep her off that conveyor belt to early sexualization.

Men, when the world starts turning too fast for your daughter, you are the best person to slow it down. Join the teddy-bear tea party. Remind her about choosing modest outfits before she even leaves for the mall. Buy her small gifts that make her feel oh-so-special. Dream today about her wedding day sometime off in the future. Help her enjoy the age and stage of life she is in right now.

Kids naturally want to grow up. Not surprisingly, your curious daughter wants to risk, to try new things, to get ahead of herself. Patience is not easy. That's why Titus 2:2 calls mature men (like you) to slow things down: "Older men are to be temperate, dignified, sensible, sound in faith, in love, in perseverance" (NASB).

And, oh yeah, while I recommend actual china for your young daughter's social affair, I am quite sure that clear, clean water is a fine substitute for tea. Nonetheless, the clink of porcelain is much to be preferred to the dull scrape of plastic teacups. Even more important, Dad, remember to sip, not slurp.

Takeaway

Sorry, Dad. Eventually you have to allow your little girl to grow up. But with your love, devotion, and guidance, she will most certainly flourish. With dignity and self-respect. With grace and humility. With virtue and significance. Just don't blink—it happens way too fast.

"We've had bad luck with our children; they've all grown up."

—CHRISTOPHER MORLEY

A Daughter Needs Her Dad…

To Understand the Power of Dopamine and Oxytocin

I am not a neuroscientist. And I'm thinking you probably are not either. But that doesn't excuse us from deciphering a couple medical terms in order to make ourselves better dads. As primary protectors of our family, sometimes we need to put in a little extra effort outside our field of expertise to keep our daughters safe. So let's put on our thinking caps for a couple pages.

Dopamine is a chemical messenger in the human brain that floods us with good feelings when we do something exciting or risky. It gives your daughter courage to venture out into the world and spread her wings. To try out for tennis. To push through the nervousness before her valedictorian speech. To say yes to a marriage proposal. These are good things. But beware—dopamine is values-neutral and can't tell right from wrong. It sends the same reward signal when our daughters experiment with drugs, alcohol, smoking, and other high-risk behaviors.

Not surprisingly, sex is one of the strongest generators of the dopamine buzz. In marriage, that's beneficial. The effect of dopamine, in a sense, "addicts" husbands and wives to each other. But outside of marriage, a young woman who has experienced a dopamine "high" will seek destructive behaviors again and again. That's why it's no surprise the Bible teaches that "marriage should be honored by all, and the marriage bed kept pure" (Hebrews 13:4).

Oxytocin is another neurochemical with powerful implications for your daughter. Primarily active in females, oxytocin produces a feeling of trust and bonding during intimate touching and sexual intercourse, causes uterine contractions at the onset of labor, and stimulates the flow of breast milk when a newborn begins to nurse. Clearly, God designed oxytocin to keep the human race reproducing and bonding within families.

But again, this chemical generated by the brain comes with a warning. The book entitled *Hooked*, by Joe S. McIlhaney, MD, and Freda McKissic Bush, MD, explains that oxytocin is also values-neutral and is generated involuntarily. It cannot tell the difference between a one-night stand and a lifelong marriage commitment:

> Oxytocin can cause a woman to bond to a man even during what was expected to be a short-term sexual relationship. She may know he is not the man she would want to marry but intimate sexual involvement causes her to be so attached to him she can't make herself separate. This can lead to a woman being taken off-guard by a desire to stay with a man she would otherwise find undesirable and staying with him even if he is possessive or abusive.[11]

In God's design, dopamine and oxytocin are generated by the brain to induce and strengthen long-term marriage relationships. Generated at the wrong time and for the wrong reasons, those chemicals can lead your daughter down a path of self-destruction. A path that literally bonds them chemically to a guy who doesn't really love them and is not their soul mate.

You and your teenage daughter already know that premarital sex can lead to unwanted pregnancy and all kinds of nasty sexually transmitted diseases. That information is out there, but today's teenagers (who think they are indestructible) think STDs and pregnancy won't happen to them. Or they mistakenly think a condom will eliminate those risks.

But the scientific truth behind dopamine and oxytocin may be new information to your daughter. If she's a romantic at heart, she might be fascinated by the idea that the feeling of being in love is supported by neurochemicals produced in the brain.

This is all one more tidbit of information you can use to inform your daughter about the downside of sex outside of marriage. Use it as you see fit. You can throw it on the pile with all the other warnings and rules you've been dumping on her. Or you could describe how science once again proves that God has a pretty good plan for how we should live our lives.

You've been telling her for years that sex should be saved for marriage. Now you can add that neurochemical bonding should also be saved for your wedding night. That may not sound very romantic, but it's scientific fact.

Takeaway

When it comes to protecting your daughter's heart, you need to come at that difficult challenge from every angle. Model the kind of husband she should look for. Warn her about the physical dangers of premarital sex. Empower her to say no. Give her candid facts and figures. Unveil the beauty and mystery of God's plan.

"It may be bizarre, but in my opinion, science offers a sure path to God and religion."

—Paul Davies

A Daughter Needs Her Dad...

To Know How Many Chapters There Are in Proverbs

There just happen to be 31 chapters in the Old Testament book of Proverbs. But you knew that, right? Well, Dad, there are also up to 31 days in a month. So let's take those two facts and use them as a way to open God's Word, connect with our daughters, and get a dose of his wisdom into their lives and ours.

This idea actually came from a good friend, Chuck, who did this every school day for years with his three daughters. On most days, his schedule allowed him to be home during the hustle of breakfast and getting his girls out the door. Standing at the toaster, leaning against the fridge, or sitting at the table, Chuck would ask the girls the date and then open to that chapter of Proverbs and read about ten verses. Then he'd ask which verse they liked best and use that proverb to inspire a short prayer for their day.

Wow. I didn't do that with my daughter. And I wish I would have. Why didn't Chuck tell me that great idea 20 years ago? We were friends back then, but it never occurred to him to tell me. And it never occurred to me to ask. I'm not angry—I'm just acknowledging a missed opportunity.

Think about the proverbs Chuck and his daughters would have covered over a dozen school years. Think about how opening the Bible became a routine and valuable way to begin their day.

On September 13, they might have read, discussed, and prayed about this verse: "A sluggard's appetite is never filled, but the desires of the diligent are fully satisfied" (Proverbs 13:4).

On February 20, they might have read, discussed, and prayed about this: "A gossip betrays a confidence; so avoid anyone who talks too much" (Proverbs 20:19).

On April 24, they might have read, discussed, and prayed about this: "An honest answer is like a kiss on the lips" (Proverbs 24:26).

They probably had some especially great discussions on the last day of October, January, May, and several other months. That's when Chuck's three daughters would have been introduced to the "Proverbs 31 Woman." You met her in an earlier chapter in this book, but Chuck's girls would have met the "wife of noble character" during a few cherished moments with their dad on a school-day morning. What a gift that was to his daughters and their future husbands.

Were there days they felt rushed? Of course. Were there days when Chuck had a business meeting, crushing deadline, or travel schedule that caused them to miss a morning? No doubt. Did he feel guilty about that? I hope not.

The only reason Chuck should feel guilty is that he didn't share this great idea with every dad he knows. Well, maybe this little chapter will make up for that.

Takeaway

Whatever works for your schedule, create a routine of Bible reading with your daughter and start this week. The key word is "routine." Or maybe the key word is "daughter." Probably the key word is "Bible." Anyway. If you find something that works for you and your daughter, tell another dad. Hey, we're all in this together.

"The fear of the LORD is the beginning of knowledge,
but fools despise wisdom and instruction."

—PROVERBS 1:7

A Daughter Needs Her Dad...

To Friend Her on Facebook

Please note. The title of this chapter is not "stalk her on Facebook" or "post something on her wall every day." When you're online, you will want to keep a respectful distance and be a reader, not a contributor. But it's your job to know what's going on in her life. In other words, Facebook is not something you should fear. It's actually a wonderful tool for parents.[12]

Of course, there's a good chance your daughter doesn't want to friend you. She's thinking worst-case scenario. Some of her friends have moms or dads who creep or lurk on social media. They comment on every post. Those parents are embarrassing their daughters and maybe even driving them to secret accounts, where they are off mom and dad's radar.

As with many parenting conundrums, you need to keep the peace and still be a welcome part of her world. In a nice, calm conversation, make these two points. Insist she friends you. Promise you won't post on her wall.

If your daughter is just launching her Facebook page, then this shouldn't be a huge problem. You bought her that laptop and smartphone. You're paying for her Internet and wireless. Tell her she cannot and should not have a presence on any social media site unless you have access to what she is sending and receiving.

If she has been on Facebook for a couple of years and claims you're intruding on her privacy, stand your ground. Keep in mind that she can control who sees what on her page, so this can be trickier than you might think. But stand firm. Again, promise you're not trying to meddle, infringe on her privacy, or crash her party. This battle of wills actually gives you another chance to pledge your commitment to protect her physical, emotional, and spiritual well-being.

If you start listing all the "bad stuff" out there, she'll accuse you of not trusting her or worrying way too much. Still, hang tough. As an informed dad, you know stalking, bullying, sexual predators, cybercrime, and other forms of online harassment are very real. You may not be able to stop the onslaught, but you are the first and best line of defense.

In his book *Teenology*, parenting authority and father of three girls, Jim Burns, encourages dads to establish a media-safe home. He reminds us that our kids are living in an era much different than when we were teenagers. He writes, "At one time the 'keep your kids in a bubble' approach might have worked, but that isn't going to happen today unless you move to a remote island, and with today's technology, that island may still have the same media choices!"[13]

Dad, as long as your daughter is under your roof and you're paying the bills, you have the right and the responsibility to have access to her wall. Prove yourself respectful and trustworthy—and perhaps even be a valued Facebook friend—and she may welcome you into her social media world after she's moved out, gone to college, or is paying her own bills. Also, don't be surprised if you get friend requests from your daughter's peers. All the while, remember, if you want to stay the cool dad, then never (or almost never) comment, share a link, or "like" anything you read on her wall.

No matter what, Dad, don't take it personally if your daughter initially tries to keep you out of her social network. A recent survey by Kaplan Test Prep found that 35 percent of teenagers ignore their parents' friending request. If that happens to you, state your case and make your expectations clear.

Worth noting. The trend is for moms to be more active on Facebook than dads. For your daughter's sake, I hope that both of her parents cruise her Facebook page once in a while to see what's going on. But, Dad, if that's not your style, you may want to leave the unobtrusive, silent monitoring up to your daughter's mom.

In a worst-case scenario, your daughter may set up her own social media account and freeze you out. If that happens, you still have options. Spyware and hacking software can get you all the information you want… and more. But aggressive surveillance techniques will put up walls between you and your daughter when really you should be building bridges. Except in extreme cases, I'm not sure I can recommend it. The goal is always to enter your daughter's world not as an enemy, but as a "friend."

Takeaway

Establishing an absolute ground rule is never easy. She may not like it, but your daughter will actually respect you for taking a firm stand on issues like Facebook. Plus, you're teaching her to take her own firm stand on even more critical issues she will face the rest of her life.

> *"One who loves a pure heart and who speaks with grace will have the king for a friend."*
>
> —Proverbs 22:11

A Daughter Needs Her Dad...

To Ask Other Dads

The real reason you're reading this book is to get ideas on how to stay connected to your daughter. That's a worthy goal. But to be honest, all I can do is share some of the things that have worked for me and my daughter. Every girl and every dad are different. What worked for me may not work for you. And vice versa.

In an attempt to expand the impact of this book (and as a ploy to have other trustworthy dads write this chapter), I asked some friends to give me specific ways in which they maintained a strong relationship with their daughter or daughters during those seasons of life when many father–daughter relationships seem to be strained.

Following are some real-life strategies. The stories were used with permission. In most cases, the names have not been changed.

Jon began reading to his daughter almost every night when she was a toddler and simply never stopped until the day she left for college. Their reading material transitioned from picture books to chapter books with more grown-up themes, including The Chronicles of Narnia, *Jesus Freaks,* and *Foxe's Book of Martyrs.* Imagine the life-changing and father-daughter-connecting conversations that took place in that bedroom over the years.

Dave and his daughter, Lauren, had a code. They liked sushi. Mom, not so much. So whenever either of them wanted to talk or just felt like going out, either one of them could say, "Hey, I feel like sushi," and they would head out on a daddy–daughter date (with mom's blessing, of course). Sometimes there was deep conversation—most of the time it was just catching up.

Ray built an impressive soccer goal in the family's backyard and volunteered often to be the practice goalie for his daughter, who eventually went on to play college soccer. Besides helping Ray stay in shape, that backyard practice area helped keep the two close even after he and his wife split up. Ray also maximized his father–daughter time in the car to and from traveling sports events.

Carl—not a wealthy guy—bought his daughter, Emily, part ownership in a real live horse. Their trips to the stable to groom and ride Pegasus have led to connection points that will last a lifetime.

Paul and his daughter, Anna, play complex strategic board games like Settlers of Catan, as well as cribbage and card games. The two admittedly have a fierce competitive streak, which leaves Mom shaking her head and smiling. The same take-no-prisoners attitude shows up when Paul takes Anna and her friends to play laser tag.

Bob has two grown daughters. Janet and Brenda have fond memories of building a rabbit cage with their dad, visiting him at work in his big downtown office building, and driving on back roads to the tiny town of Footville, Wisconsin, while learning the family history.

Finally, I asked my brother Mark how he has always stayed so wonderfully connected to his three beautiful, creative, and amusing young adult daughters. In his own humble way, he took no credit. But Becky, Stephanie, and Alyssa revealed the family secret—it's their love of music, in all its forms.

According to his daughters, Mark has the gift to spontaneously rewrite lyrics to popular songs with decidedly absurd and disarming results. Hang around my nieces long enough and you'll hear "I Believe I Like Pie," sung to the tune of "I Believe I Can Fly." Or you might hear made-up lyrics telling the entire Christmas story, sung to show tunes from *Hello, Dolly*. I understand song reimagining was especially popular during cross-country car trips.

When his daughter Steph quit piano lessons after four years, it was disappointing to Mark, but not tragic. A few months later, when he heard her say something about really liking the music in the film *The Man from Snowy River*, he ran out and picked up the sheet music for the soundtrack. As a result, Steph picked up piano again and is still enjoying it ten years later.

Even longer ago, Becky and some of her preteen friends were part of that generation of girls who were quite enamored with the Backstreet Boys. To his credit, Mark surprised her with four concert tickets. Becky and two of her girlfriends (and Mark) attended a concert they will never forget. That boisterous event gives new meaning to the idea of "entering your daughter's world."

So Dad, those are some ideas you may want to adapt as your own. Really, there's nothing magic going on here. It's just regular guys being a little creative with a rock-solid consistency. It's not difficult. Find something you and your daughter both like—sushi, board games, reading, silly songs. Invite her to enter your world—at your place of work or the town where you grew up. Build something together—a soccer goal or rabbit cage. Help your daughter set and reach a personal goal—college soccer, learning piano. If you're really looking to connect, buy her a rabbit or even a horse. Or maybe even take her to a boy-band concert with a couple of her friends.

Thanks, men—you've given all of us some new ideas and you've written one fifty-second of this book. I owe each of you lunch. And congratulations for raising such fine young ladies.

Takeaway

Stay tight with a group of guys who can support each other in your fathering efforts. Be intentional about sharing ideas and knowing what other dads and daughters in your area are doing.

> *"It can be unsettling to be the father of a teenage or young-adult daughter. But don't shirk your responsibilities. Prepare her. Do the best you can, and then stay on your knees. And you may find, like we did, that there are great benefits."*
>
> —Carey Casey

A Daughter Needs Her Dad…

To Help Her Experience the Great Exchange Early

To describe what Jesus did on the cross, theologians use the term *substitutionary atonement*. That's a fancy way of saying that we've all sinned, that each of us deserves punishment for those sins, but that Jesus paid that price for each of us when he died on the cross.

Three passages from the Bible make it clear.

> Surely he took up our pain and bore our suffering, yet we considered him punished by God, stricken by him, and afflicted. But he was pierced for our transgressions, he was crushed for our iniquities; the punishment that brought us peace was on him, and by his wounds we are healed. We all, like sheep, have gone astray, each of us has turned to our own way; and the LORD has laid on him the iniquity of us all (Isaiah 53:4-6).

> God made him who had no sin to be sin for us, so that in him we might become the righteousness of God (2 Corinthians 5:21).

> "He himself bore our sins" in his body on the cross, so that we might die to sins and live for righteousness; "by his wounds you have been healed" (1 Peter 2:24).

Do you get it? Jesus loved us so much that he took our place. One of my favorite terms for this act is "the Great Exchange." That paints an accurate picture of my inferior self being replaced by a new righteousness. The "old me" was nailed up on that cross and exchanged for a "new person."

All our children need to know this. And perhaps your most important job as their father is to establish an environment in which they each understand and accept that free gift of grace. But daughters especially need to be reminded of this truth early and often.

You see, just about every girl is going to pass through a phase in which she feels worthless. Boys not so much. Boys almost do the opposite—feeling indestructible or invincible. For dads raising young men, that leads to an entire different set of challenges. But when it comes to your daughter, you'll want to make sure she has a solid, committed understanding of her identity as a new creation in Christ when she first experiences those feelings of worthlessness.

When her peers are agonizing over self-image and inferiority, your daughter will be able to say—or think—"I am worth Jesus." If she has been living with God's grace for more than a few years, there's a good chance your daughter may slide through that murky period of her life with a little less angst and self-doubt. During those early years, you can help by intentionally and sincerely pointing out how God has been working in her life. Anticipate moments when she shows compassion to a friend, patience with a sibling, or generosity with a stranger.

Let her know when you see God's love reflected in her words and actions. This isn't false praise or artificial self-esteem-building, which ultimately falls flat. As a new creation, your daughter will literally have new gifts and points of view that she may not even realize she has. Think about the response of the servants in Jesus' story when the King gives them his thanks and blessing for feeding, visiting, clothing, and caring for him. They were confused. They said, "Lord, when did we see you hungry and feed you, or thirsty and give you something to drink? When did we see you a stranger and invite you in, or needing clothes and clothe you? When did we see you sick or in prison and go to visit you?" (Matthew 25:37-39). That righteous bunch didn't know the magnitude of their good deeds. They didn't know that they had been renewed from the inside out by their relationship with Jesus.

Dad, you are the best person to witness and point out how Christ has transformed your little girl's life. You know the before and after. You are in a unique position to help her see how valuable she is. Make sure she experiences, celebrates, and cherishes the Great Exchange.

Takeaway

In this case, what's good for your daughter is good for every member of your family. Including you, Dad.

> *"If anyone is in Christ, the new creation has*
> *come: The old has gone, the new is here!"*
>
> —2 CORINTHIANS 5:17

A Daughter Needs Her Dad...

To Be Ready for Anything During Middle School

Your daughter will survive her middle-school years. You might not. But if you've helped her establish some moral convictions and you display a little confidence in her abilities, she might just surprise you. On her own, she will figure out who she needs to be, what she needs to do, and how she needs to act to maneuver through the minefields of sixth, seventh, and eighth grades. Without question, she will need to endure a certain amount of anguish and frustration. A little is good, a lot is not.

As usual, Rae Anne supplies several excellent examples.

About those little volleyball shorts. She made the team. She developed a strong serve. At the end of the year, she even won the "Kamikaze Award" for her willingness to sacrifice herself diving after loose volleyballs just to save a point. But when they passed out the skimpy black shorts that are standard issue for most high-school teams, Rae said no thanks and opted for black gym shorts. As far as I know, no one teased her for taking her own stand for modesty. It was a decision she made on her own, and she had earned that right because she worked hard in practice and played hard in games.

The nondancing dance chairman. Rae Anne knows how to dance. She loves music. She's coordinated and in tune with cultural norms. Once in a while, she and I dance in the kitchen. But in middle school, she was shy about dancing in public. That's not unusual and it wasn't a problem. But that left Rita and me a little confused when Rae Anne told us she was the chairman for the upcoming eighth-grade dance. We volunteered to chaperone and wondered what the evening would bring. As we watched from a respectful distance, Rae kept busy all night monitoring the ticket booth, food and beverage tables, and other activities. Our resourceful daughter had found her own way to go to a dance and have a great time, without dancing.

More than a wrestling fan. By the time Rae Anne was in middle school, she had watched literally thousands of wrestling matches. Every winter for as long as she could remember, her four older brothers practiced moves in our living room and basement, talked wrestling strategy, and watched wrestling videos. Of course, wrestling is a boys' sport, but every once in a while a girl insists on joining a middle- or high-school team. When that happens the integrity of the sport suffers. Without any warning, that girl's male opponents are forced to make a choice they shouldn't have to make. If a boy forfeits the match, he lets the team down. If he wrestles the girl possessing all the standard girl body parts, he doesn't feel comfortable using many of the holds and pinning combinations he's been practicing.

To be sure, Rae Anne would have made a pretty good wrestler, but she never even considered it. Instead she supported the boys on her middle-school team any way she could. In the stands, as an athletic trainer, keeping the clock, even mat-side coaching of inexperienced wrestlers. When picking her up from a wrestling tournament one day, I couldn't locate her in the gym. After searching all the typical spots, I found her working as an official scorer, which was normally a paid position reserved for adults. It turns out the scoring was too complicated for the assigned teacher, who kept requesting help from Rae Anne. Finally, the teacher just slid the scorebook over and hired my daughter for the day. She made $30.

Latent musical genius. Near the end of the year, the eighth-graders take over the high-school theater auditorium for what they call a talent show. Supposedly they actually require the student acts to audition, but I'm pretty sure they let anyone participate who signs up. The real purpose of the audition is to decide the order of the acts. They attempt to get the not-so-slick acts over with early and save the best for last. Well, guess who was last? Our Rae Anne! And guess what she did? Sang and played an original song on the piano!

Why do I seem surprised? Because until that moment I hadn't known she could sing or play the piano. Sure, I'd heard her banging out some chords and humming to herself at our living-room piano. But that night, she blew away the audience and totally deserved the standing ovation that was still thundering when she exited the stage. I'm still not sure where that poise and that voice came from, but the entire experience was one of those revelations we fathers need once in a while to remind us that we still have much to learn about our own kids. (I'd post the video for you to see on YouTube, but Rae refuses.)

So that's four snapshots of my daughter in middle school. In a way, it's four different girls standing their ground and finding their way. It all adds up to the woman she is today. And that doesn't even include the youth events and Bible studies at church. Which, thinking back, were probably even more important than I realized.

As for me, those three years are mostly a blur. Thankfully, I can still pick out a handful of specific moments with absolute clarity. I can close my eyes and she's right there. I'm so glad I was there for those moments.

Takeaway

Your 12-year-old daughter might say she loves school one day. And hates it the next. Both days she's lying. And that's okay.

> *"When I was in middle school, some of my so-called friends found a catalogue ad I did for Superman pajamas. They made as many copies as they could and pasted them up all over school."*
>
> —JENSEN ACKLES

A Daughter Needs Her Dad...

To Share a Secret Banana Split

I'm not sure what a licensed psychologist would say about this, but I'm going to say it anyway.

Little girls (and big girls and wives and just about all women) have body-image issues. An earlier chapter gave you some scientific research about anorexia, bulimia, and other food battles. But the following two suggestions are not based on any million-dollar studies or laboratory research. They come from the heart of a dad who just wants every little girl to know her daddy loves her just the way she is. Ready?

1. Never, ever say or imply that your daughter is fat.

2. When you're out running errands, once or twice a year take her for a secret banana split.

If you don't know where I'm coming from, allow me to explain. The entire world is telling your daughter that she cannot be happy unless she loses some weight. As her daddy, you are the only person in the world who can successfully counter that erroneous and evil attack.

This means you can't say quite a few of the things you believe are harmless or even helpful. Because they *do* harm and they *don't* help. Examples: "Are you getting enough exercise?" "Why don't you eat an apple instead?" "It's funny how your sister can eat so much and not put on any weight." "Did you know there are 140 calories in a can of Coke?" "My Aunt Ruth was overweight."

None of these sound like an attack. But if they come out of your mouth, your lovely, sweet, and perfect little girl is going to hear this: "Daughter, you're fat." If that sounds harsh, that's because it is harsh. Very harsh. If you don't believe me, ask your wife.

The banana-split idea is simply a way to build up an immunity to anything stupid you might say. A father and daughter stopping at Dairy Queen is a tasty and unspoken way to remind your daughter to not obsess over food. Keeping your ice-cream rendezvous a secret from Mom and any siblings helps make it an even more positive experience. A therapist might say that any "food secret" is a bad thing. Or they might say that associating ice cream with an outing with your father is dangerous. And I see their point. The issue is highly flammable.

On the other hand, I think a secret banana split shared between a dad and his daughter on a hot August day is really saying, "You and me, we're pals. The heck with what the world says. I'm awesome. You're awesome. Let's make sure we do this once every summer for the next five or six decades!"

Doesn't that sound like a conversation you want to have?

Takeaway

A few daddy–daughter secrets are a good thing. It could be a secret fishing spot or a charm for her bracelet that has special meaning to just the two of you. It could be paying cash for a pair of $90 jeans that Mom said were too expensive. It could be a secret wink, earlobe tug, or nose scrunch known only to you and your daughter. Got a daddy–daughter secret? If not, share one today.

> *"Even the models we see in magazines wish they*
> *could look like their own images."*
>
> —CHERI K. ERDMAN

A Daughter Needs Her Dad…

To Be Whittling on the Front Porch When the Suitors Come Calling

Got a shotgun? Get one. Because teenage boys need to know you are serious about protecting your precious daughter.

When the boys start coming around, you need to be conspicuous in your presence. You need those rascals to know that the girl they want to kiss (and more) has a dad who would die for her. And maybe kill for her.

Now, you don't want to scare them off. Truthfully, you want them to come to your porch and ring your doorbell. You want your home to be a place where your daughter can invite a boy over to watch a PG-13 movie, play Scrabble, shoot pool, or even sit and talk football with you on a Sunday afternoon. You want to know who they are, what motivates them, and a little about their hopes and dreams. If you go a little overboard with your quizzing, that's actually a good thing. Your daughter might tell you later, "Daddy, your interrogation of Andrew was totally embarrassing." But secretly she's glad you care so much.

From the outside looking in, teenage boys, cat burglars, con men, and cult members should recognize your piece of property as a fortress of truth and virtue. Anyone looking for a warm, loving environment filled with good conversation, laughter, and mutual respect is welcome. Anyone with selfish or evil intentions had better move on.

Dads set boundaries. Good dads protect them fiercely. Great dads equip their daughter to set her own personal boundaries.

And that's one of the most important truths in this chapter and this book. Your little girl is not always going to be living in your home under your watchful eye, protected by your hunting knife and 12-gauge. She needs to see herself as tremendously valuable and worth protecting. She needs to know that you will be her champion and knight in shining armor. But when you're not around, she needs to have her own plan for protecting herself. And yes, I'm talking about rape, date rape, aggressive boyfriends, creepy stalkers, and any guy who cares more about himself than about her.

Without words, you can model how men should treat a lady. Without words, your daughter's mom should set an example of carrying herself with modesty and confidence. But the best way to instill the necessary self-protection strategies is by having a good old-fashioned conversation. It might begin as a lecture and that's okay, but you will want to actually dialogue about why, when, and how your daughter can protect herself from the mistakes made by so many teenage girls today.

Before she starts dating, your young daughter needs to hear that

1. she has value

2. her virginity is worth protecting

3. boys think about sex a lot

4. it's really easy for her to send the wrong signals

5. sex is not the same as love

6. boys think about sex a lot

7. safe sex is a myth

8. STDs are epidemic among young people

9. she shouldn't go to places where guys are looking for one-night stands

10. she can say no and mean it

11. boys think about sex a lot

12. if she has already gone too far, she can still get a new start

13. she must decide early and often that she is going to save herself for marriage

There's a lot to cover. But it's all important. Each of these concepts is worthy of its own chapter or book. New research continues to reveal the physical, emotional, spiritual, and pleasure advantages of a monogamous long-term marriage relationship. That begins not at an altar, but with an attitude she chooses well before her first date. You can help instill that attitude by having one or more of those not-so-easy conversations.

Finally, Dad, in many ways boys and girls haven't changed since you were a teenager. But you may not be aware of a recent trend toward sexual aggressiveness from girls toward guys. That makes this whole issue even a little scarier. And all the more important. With or without your shotgun, you are the first and best line of defense.

Takeaway

If you don't know how to begin this conversation with your daughter, go ahead and open this book to this page and ask her what she thinks about the above 13 points. Especially don't forget to mention, "Boys think about sex a lot."

> *"A father…knows exactly what those boys at the mall have in their depraved little minds because he once owned such a depraved little mind himself. In fact, if he thinks enough about the plans that he used to have for young girls, the father not only will support his wife in keeping their daughter home but he might even run over to the mall and have a few of those boys arrested."*
>
> —BILL COSBY

A Daughter Needs Her Dad…

To Ask Her Questions
She Wants You to Ask

I'm good friends with the team at the National Center for Fathering. I can't say enough about the impact they've made on my life and perhaps millions of other men and their kids. Their website—fathers.com—has info on all kinds of events, programs, and resources. If you have school-age kids, check out their Watch D.O.G.S. program. Maybe you can convince your daughter to nominate you for their official Fathering Hall of Fame. CEO Carey Casey has been invited to fathering summits at the White House on your behalf, and he delivers inspiring messages at churches and men's gatherings all across the country. After 20 years, I'm still actively involved in writing and producing their daily three-minute radio broadcast, *Today's Father*, which airs on more than 400 stations.

The Center schedules a variety of workshops and training events throughout the year, including Championship Fathering seminars, Train the Trainer programs, and Father–Daughter Summits. To add to their significant bank of research, they interviewed a significant sampling of young women (ages 13–24) and asked a series of questions. One of those questions really stuck out to me because it revealed new insight you and I can really use. The question was this: "What are two questions your dad could ask you to demonstrate that he really cares about what's going on in your life?"

The answers were surprising, because I would think most girls do *not* want their fathers to pester them with a bunch of nosey questions about their life and their day-to-day activities. Well, Dad. It seems just the opposite is true.

As reported by Brock Griffin of the National Center for Fathering, the most common responses fell into four categories:

1. Daughters desired a *daily review*. They actually wanted to be asked questions like: "What happened at school today?" "How's it going?" "Did everything go well with your friends today?" "Did any bad things happen today?" One young lady added, "After asking how my day went, it helps if he maintains eye contact and waits for the answer."

2. Daughters wanted their dads to ask specific questions about the *boys or young men in their lives*. "How old is the guy you want to go out with?" "How are guys treating you at school?" "Are you being pressured sexually by any guy?" "How is your love life or lack of a love life?" One daughter elaborated: "Dad kind of assumes everything is going well and he rarely asks questions about my guy friends."

3. Daughters hoped their dads would ask questions that had *emotional implications*. These included questions like "Do you know how much I love you?" "How are you doing lately as far as emotional stuff?" "Are you upset about anything?" "How are you feeling?"

4. Lastly, these girls were actually eager to answer questions related to *their future and their faith*: "What are your goals?" "What are you thinking about your future?" "What is God showing you?" "How are your spiritual life, your quiet times, and your relationship with God?"

This is a little stunning, don't you think? Just when your growing daughter appears ready to move on without your oppressive interrogations, the opposite is true. Again, these are not questions thought up by curious, overbearing, or overprotective dads. These are questions actually written down by teenage and twentysomething daughters. The National

Center for Fathering is a research-based organization. They don't make this stuff up.

My spin is this. Your growing daughter will not tell you this stuff out of the blue. She is waiting for you to ask. She wants you to initiate the dialogue. When you ask her personal questions, she feels loved, protected, and secure.

Taking it a step further. Because she knows you're going to ask about her day and her life, she might consciously make better choices along the way. Once again, Dad, you matter.

Worth noting. I asked my 20-year-old daughter, Rae Anne, if she wanted me to ask her the above questions on a regular basis. She knew the response I was fishing for. So of course she looked at me and said, "Well, Dad, don't ask me anything you don't want to know the answer to."

Hmm. I guess that means I need to wait a few days and rephrase those questions before I ask.

Takeaway

You absolutely care about every aspect of your daughter's life. From grades to friends to romance. From her frustrations today to her future tomorrow. Does she know that? Does she know how much you really care? Asking her heartfelt questions is really a way of saying, "Daughter, my love for you overflows beyond all measure."

> *"There's something like a line of gold thread running through a man's words when he talks to his daughter, and gradually over the years it gets to be long enough for you to pick up in your hands and weave into a cloth that feels like love itself."*
>
> —John Gregory Brown

A Daughter Needs Her Dad...

To Expect Her Claws to Come Out Once in a While

have three lovely daughters-in-law. Rachel, Lindsay, Megan.

(And, by the way, many of the principles and ideas in this book can be applied to dealing with the girl who marries your son.)

Anyway. Back in 2008, everyone in our family was undeniably looking forward to the first wedding of any of my kids. Randall had proposed to Rachel. She had said yes. And she would change her name to Payleitner that fall. My wife, my other three sons, and I were joyously anticipating gaining a wonderful addition to the family. Rae Anne not so much.

Rae Anne, 15 at the time, was secretly not looking forward to the idea of breaking up her gang. She liked having four brothers. She liked being the only girl. And she didn't want anyone messing with the chemistry of her family. That feeling had nothing really to do with Rachel. To Rae Anne's credit, there wasn't a violent display of cattiness or meanness. Her undercurrent of resentment remained secret to everyone except my own bride. Rita knows her daughter, and she sensed something was amiss and stayed silently vigilant for any possible friction during that summer before the wedding. There was no confrontation or showdown. My daughter was smart enough to never say or do anything she would regret later.

The outdoor October wedding was beautiful. Rae Anne was an elegant bridesmaid. And in the months that followed a wonderful thing happened. Rae saw that instead of breaking up the family, the addition of a sister-in-law actually made the Payleitners stronger. For the first time, she had a big sister. It really didn't take long before my daughter and daughter-in-law became the best of friends, seeking each other's company even when no males were present.

Dad here—who was oblivious to the entire summer of one-sided animosity—was totally surprised when the truth came out. As we sat around our kitchen table one Sunday afternoon not long ago, Rae Anne admitted, "Oh yeah, I hated Rachel for about a year." Everyone at the table laughed, but I was stunned. All I could think of was, *What would have happened if my daughter had proclaimed that hatred a week before the wedding?* Yikes.

All that to say, just when you think you know your daughter, she'll surprise you. Plus, dads should realize that girls will protect their turf differently than boys. Guys will figuratively or literally draw a line in the dirt and dare their adversary to cross it. Girls may appear to be BFFs one minute and turn wildcat the next. Thankfully that hasn't happened in my growing family. Yet.

Takeaway

There are very likely subtexts and undercurrents in your daughter's life you don't even realize. If and when they rise to the surface, stand ready to intercede and assist as necessary. But rather than try to figure out every possible emotion or thought she might have, it's probably easier and wiser to expect some kind of emotions to flare up every once in a while. With her mother's help, I'm confident you'll respond with patience, composure, and discretion. Right, Dad?

"Women are made to be loved, not understood."

—Oscar Wilde

A Daughter Needs Her Dad...

To Let Her Go

My daughter is currently attending West Point. The United States Military Academy. That's an eleven-year commitment. Four years of college. Five years of active duty. And two years in the Reserve.

I don't want to get ahead of Rae Anne's assignments and deployments, but there's a good chance she'll stick around in the US Army beyond those years. And when she does leave the military, there's a good chance her life and career path may lead someplace other than her Midwest hometown. When Rae does come home, we delight in every day we can spend with her. But when the break, holiday, or furlough is over, we have to let her go all over again. And that's usually not very easy.

How did this West Point adventure come about? It also wasn't easy. The admissions process was initiated by 13,954 applicants, 4344 then received congressional nominations, 2540 qualified academically and physically, and only 1261 were admitted. Of those admitted, 97 were valedictorians, 747 were members of the National Honor Society, and 777 were captains on a varsity athletic team.

My wife, Rita, and I did not know Rae Anne was even considering West Point until just before her junior year of high school. Because she wanted to play Division I softball, we spent much of that summer traveling to exposure tournaments and showcases around the Midwest. She had gotten some looks, but the highly structured college recruitment process is all about contacting the right coaches and showing off the right stuff at the right time. At these events, parents are not allowed to initiate conversations with any college coaches, so all Rita and I could do was watch, cheer, and hope.

At a St. Louis tournament, we noticed a coach with ARMY on her jacket taking notes behind the backstop when Rae Anne was catching. We assumed she was scouting the pitcher. But after an inning or two, it became apparent the Army coach was paying close attention to our daughter working behind the plate. After the game, she chatted briefly with Rae Anne. "What was that all about?" we asked later. "That's the West Point coach—I invited her," was my daughter's matter-of-fact response. News to us.

After two anxious years and jumping through a hundred hoops, Rae Anne reported for duty at West Point just three weeks after high school graduation. On R-Day, there's a moment when incoming plebes and parents are ushered into an auditorium for a brief instructional talk and then, on command, the young people are given 90 seconds to say good-bye to their moms and dads. We had been warned. We knew it was coming. Quick, sturdy hugs, final gasping words of love, and wiped tears filled the room. Stunned parents watched their sons and daughters line up with surprising efficiency and then shuffle with a mix of confidence and uncertainty through a metal door to meet their future.

We let her go. Not the first time. Nor the last.

That's what dads do. We get them ready to leave. We lay the sleeping baby in a bassinet and tiptoe out of the nursery. We watch her line up for the first day of kindergarten. We drop them off at a sleepover across town. We put them on the bus to youth camp. We carry laundry baskets up three flights of stairs to a freshman dorm. We walk them down the aisle on their wedding day. We let their mom have the last hug on R-Day. That's what dads do.

As we looked around the much emptier auditorium, tears filled the eyes of every single parent. Funny, though. Moms tilt their heads down, remembering the past. Dads hold their heads up, envisioning the future.

That's what dads do.

Takeaway

Be there, Dad. When your little girl looks around for her daddy, you be there. But when the time comes, help your daughter understand that it's really okay for her to make her own way. To trust God. To trust what you've taught her. To see a future filled with love, faith, joy, and purpose.

"I love you, Rae Anne. You're on your way."

—DAD

Notes

1. Janet Shibley Hyde, "The Gender Similarities Hypothesis," *American Psychologist,* September 2005 (vol. 60, no. 6), pp. 581-592.

2. Meg Meeker, *Strong Fathers, Strong Daughters* (New York: Ballantine Books, 2007), pp. 129-130.

3. This chapter is adapted from Jay Payleitner, *52 Things Kids Need from a Dad* (Eugene, OR: Harvest House Publishers, 2010), pp. 133-135.

4. Sources are respectively as follows: The National Eating Disorders Association; L. Mellin et al., "A longitudinal study of the dietary practices of black and white girls 9 and 10 years old at enrollment: The NHLBI growth and health study," *Journal of Adolescent Health*, 1991, pp. 23-37; The Renfrew Center Foundation for Eating Disorders, "Eating Disorders 101 Guide: A Summary of Issues, Statistics and Resources," 2003; Renfrew Center.

5. The following points are taken from Joe S. McIlhaney Jr. and Freda McKissic Bush, *Girls Uncovered: New Research on What America's Sexual Culture Does to Young Women* (Chicago: Northfield Publishing, 2011), respectively, pp. 37, 41, 46, 54.

6. McIlhaney and Bush, p. 56.

7. Sources are respectively as follows: www.acenet.edu/AM/Template.cfm?Section=Home&CON TENTID=35338&TEMPLATE=/CM/ContentDisplay.cfm; National Center for Education Statistics, "Projections of Education Statistics by 2016," Tables 27-31, http://nces.ed.gov/pro grams/projections/projections2016/tables.asp#t27; http://womeninbusiness.about.com/od/ womeninbusinessnew1/a/decade-women-ceos.htm; http://abcnews.go.com/blogs/business/2011/10/ record-number-of-fortune-500-women-ceos/.

8. www.forbes.com/2006/02/08/best-selling-cosmetics_cx_me_0209feat_ls.html.

9. Sources are respectively as follows: http://today.msnbc.msn.com/id/26182276/#.UBrUZUQzJbQ; http://foreverfamilies.byu.edu/Article.aspx?a=159; http://www.usatoday.com/news/health/ wellness/story/2011/04/Parents-decry-marketers-who-push-sexuality-on-little-girls/46021496/1.

10. Drawn from Dannah Gresh, *Six Ways to Keep the "Little" in Your Girl* (Eugene, OR: Harvest House Publishers, 2010), p. 144.

11. Joe S. McIlhaney Jr. and Freda McKissic Bush, *Hooked: New Science on How Casual Sex Is Affecting Our Children* (Chicago: Northfield Publishing, 2008), p. 38.

12. http://digitallife.today.msnbc.msn.com/_news/2012/04/24/11374466-60-percent-of-us-parents-spy-on-teens-facebook-accounts-survey?lite.

13. Jim Burns, *Teenology: The Art of Raising Great Teenagers* (Grand Rapids, MI: Bethany House, 2010), pp. 62-63.

Books by Jay Payleitner

Once Upon a Tandem

The One Year Life Verse Devotional

52 Things Kids Need from a Dad

365 Ways to Say "I Love You" to Your Kids

52 Things Wives Need from Their Husbands

One-Minute Devotions for Dads

If God Gave Your Graduation Speech

52 Things Daughters Need from Their Dads

About the Author

Jay Payleitner is a dad. But he pays his mortgage and feeds his family working as a freelance writer, ad man, motivational speaker and radio producer with credits including *Josh McDowell Radio*, *WordPower*, *Jesus Freaks Radio*, and *Today's Father with Carey Casey*. Jay served as the Executive Director for the Illinois Fatherhood Initiative and is a featured writer/blogger for the National Center for Fathering. He is also a best-selling author. Jay and his high-school sweetheart, Rita, have four sons, one daughter, and three daughters-in-law and live in St. Charles, Illinois. You can read his weekly dadblog at jaypayleitner.com.

The National Center for Fathering

We believe *every* child needs a dad they can count on. At the National Center for Fathering, we inspire and equip men to be the involved fathers, stepfathers, grandfathers, and father figures their children need.

The National Center was founded by Dr. Ken Canfield in 1990 as a non-profit scientific and education organization. Today, under the leadership of CEO Carey Casey, we continue to provide practical, research-based training and resources that reach more than one million dads annually.

We focus our work in four areas, all of which are described in detail at fathers.com:

Research. The Personal Fathering Profile, developed by a team of researchers led by Ken Canfield, and other ongoing research projects provide fresh insights for fathers and serve as benchmarks for evaluating the effectiveness of our programs and resources.

Training. Through Championship Fathering Experiences, Father–Daughter Summits, online training, small-group curricula, and train-the-trainer programs, we have equipped over 80,000 fathers and more than 1000 trainers to impact their own families and local communities.

Programs. The National Center provides leading edge, turnkey fathering programs, including WATCH D.O.G.S. (Dads Of Great Students), which involves dads in their children's education and is currently in more than 1300 schools in 36 states. Other programs include Fathering Court, which helps dads with significant child-support arrearages, and our annual Father of the Year Essay Contest.

Resources. Our website provides a wealth of resources for dads in nearly every fathering situation, many of them available free of charge. Dads who make a commitment to Championship Fathering receive a free weekly e-newsletter full of timely and practical tips on fathering. *Today's Father*, Carey Casey's daily radio program, airs on 600-plus stations. Listen to programs online or download podcasts at fathers.com/radio.

Make your commitment to Championship Fathering

Championship Fathering is an effort to change the culture for today's children and the children of coming generations. We're seeking to reach, teach, and unleash 6.5 million dads, creating a national movement of men who will commit to LOVE their children, COACH their children, MODEL for their children, ENCOURAGE other children, and ENLIST other dads to join the team. To make the Championship Fathering commitment, visit fathers.com/cf.

Also by Jay Payleitner

52 Things Kids Need from a Dad
What Fathers Can Do to Make a Lifelong Difference

Good news—you are already the perfect dad for your kids! Still, you know you can grow. In the pages of this bestseller, Jay Payleitner, veteran radio producer and dad of five, offers a bounty of inspiring and unexpected insights:

- *straightforward rules*: "carry photos of your kids," "Dad tucks in," and "kiss your wife in the kitchen"

- *candid advice that may be tough to hear*: "get right with your own dad," "throw out your porn," and "surrender control of the TV remote"

- *weird topics that at first seem absurd*: "buy Peeps," "spin a bucket over your head" and "rent a dolphin"

Surely, God—our heavenly Father—designed fatherhood to be a joy, a blessing, and a blast! *A great gift or men's group resource.*

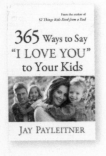

365 Ways to Say "I Love You" to Your Kids

Expressions of love can get lost in the crush of carpools, diaper changes, homework, and afterschool activities. But Jay Payleitner is here to help you turn the dizzying array of activities into great memories. Learn to say "I love you"…

> …*at bedtime…in the car…in different languages… without words…doing chores…when your kids mess up big time…on vacation…using secret phrases…in crazy unexpected ways…in everyday life…in ways that point to God.*

Whether your kids are newborn or college-bound, these 365 simple suggestions—from silly to serious—will help you lead your precious pack to joy, laughter, and connection one "I love you" at a time.

52 Things Wives Need from Their Husbands
What Husbands Can Do to Build a Stronger Marriage

Nobody knows your wife like you do. You're the guy who can make her day or break her heart. The choice is yours. If you feel your husband technique could use a quick refresher course, look no further. Jay Payleitner, husband of Rita and veteran dad of five, offers a bounty of man-friendly advice, such as

- "Surprise her with sparkly gifts"
- "Be the handyman"
- "Stay married"
- "Kiss her in the kitchen"
- "Leave your mommy"
- "Push the right buttons"

From breakfast to bedtime. For newlyweds to empty-nesters. Here's a great and godly start to winning your wife's heart all over again!

"Biblical, fun, wise, and refreshing...Get it and you'll thank me for having told you about it."

—**Steve Brown**
author, professor, and radio teacher on Key Life

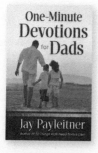

One-Minute Devotions for Dads

Lots of dads feel a twinge of terror at the word *devotion.* Something dull and guilt-producing. Something you're supposed to read at 5 a.m. before you do your 100 push-ups and eat your bowl of oat bran.

Enter Jay Payleitner, exit terror. A veteran dad, Jay knows how regular guys think because he is one. His Bible-based coaching sessions—devotions, if you must—offer you unexpected but relevant thoughts and touches of offbeat humor. And "What About You?" wrap-ups leave you with something straightforward to do or think about.

Young dads, older dads—your day will get a shot in the arm from Jay's seasoned wisdom and God-centered thinking.

Other Helpful Resources from Harvest House

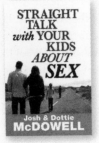

Straight Talk with Your Kids About Sex
Josh and Dottie McDowell

If your kids are going to get the message about God's plan for sex, you're the right choice to give it. Statistics show they listen to you and *want* to hear from you. It's not easy, but Josh and Dottie McDowell make it very doable. This compact, easy-to-use guide will help you

- put sex and sexuality in a biblical context of relationship to God
- be alert to questions and opportunities
- form a positive foundation for your kids' lives as you relate to them and dream with them about their future

Quick "tips and ideas" chapters add an extra boost, giving you confidence and solid, up-to-date information for the sometimes-awkward process of guiding your kids into a healthy understanding of God's gift of sex.

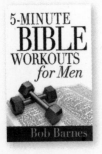

5-Minute Bible Workouts for Men
Bob Barnes

Is the pressure getting to you? Where can you turn to find relief?

With demands that constantly call for your attention, it's easy to skip out on your time with God.

If you'd like to change that, *5-Minute Bible Workouts for Men* is for you. Each devotion takes less than five minutes to read and offers valuable direction, wisdom, and encouragement that can strengthen you, your relationships, and your walk with God.

5-Minute Bible Workouts for Men is an excellent tool for maximizing your time with God. Start your day with a one-on-one workout with Him, and you'll be energized all day long.

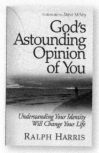

God's Astounding Opinion of You

Understanding Your Identity Will Change Your Life
Ralph Harris

Do you know that God's view of you is much greater than your own? Ralph Harris, founder and President of Life-Course Ministries, leads you to embrace the Scriptures' truth about what God thinks of you—that you are special to Him, blameless, and pure, and He respects and loves you.

With clear and simple explanations and examples, this resource will help you turn toward the friendship with God you were created for…a relationship in which you

- exchange fear and obligation for delight and devotion
- recognize the remarkable role and strength of the Holy Spirit in your daily life
- view your status as a *new creation* as the "new normal"— and live accordingly!

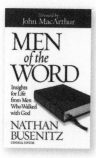

Men of the Word

Insights for Life from Men Who Walked with God
Nathan Busenitz, general editor

"A must-read for any man who desires to grow in godliness."
—John MacArthur

What is God's calling for men? What character qualities does He value? What is biblical manhood, and how is it cultivated?

You'll find the answers to these all-important questions in the lives of the men of the Bible—men like Abraham, David, Nehemiah, Paul, and Timothy. Every one of them struggled with the same issues men like you face today. From them, you'll learn that real men…

live by faith	treasure God's Word
pray with boldness	flee temptation
love to worship	refuse to compromise
lead with courage	find satisfaction in God

Take the challenge to become all God wants you to be. His Word shows you the way. *Includes study guide.*

To learn more about Harvest House books and
to read sample chapters, log on to our website:

www.harvesthousepublishers.com

HARVEST HOUSE PUBLISHERS
EUGENE, OREGON